30-MINUTE GROUPS

GRIEF

PROCESSING EMOTIONS, HONORING MEMORIES, AND FINDING HOPE

MAKENZIE PERKINS

NATIONAL CENTER for
YOUTH ISSUES

Duplication and Copyright

No part of this publication may be reproduced, stored in a retrieval system, or transmitted in any form by any means, electronic, mechanical, photocopy, video or audio recording, or otherwise without prior written permission from the publisher, except for all worksheets and activities which may be reproduced for a specific group or class. Reproduction for an entire school or school district is prohibited.

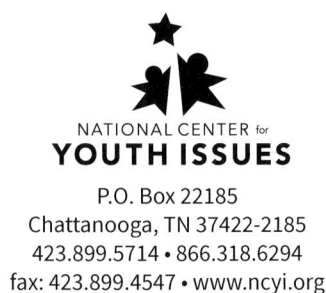

NATIONAL CENTER for YOUTH ISSUES

P.O. Box 22185
Chattanooga, TN 37422-2185
423.899.5714 • 866.318.6294
fax: 423.899.4547 • www.ncyi.org

ISBN: 9781965066034

© 2024 National Center for Youth Issues, Chattanooga, TN

All rights reserved.

Written by: Makenzie Perkins, M.S.

Published by National Center for Youth Issues

Printed in the U.S.A. • November 2024

Contents

Introduction

Loss is a universal experience that can profoundly impact a child's development and life experiences. The *30-Minute Groups: Grief* small-group curriculum consists of ten to twelve thirty-minute sessions to help students process their loss and grow around their grief. **Our goal with this curriculum is to help create a safe place for children to share their unique experiences with grief, while also empowering them with tools that promote emotional healing and resilience.**

The grief curriculum is designed for students in grades 2 through 8. It helps students process a variety of different losses, including death. In many settings, students avoid conversations about loss and grief or meet them with discomfort and uncertainty. This curriculum recognizes that many people feel unsure how to support someone grieving and equips facilitators with an easy-to-use, no-prep resource to help guide students through loss. Acknowledging that every response to loss is unique, the curriculum is adaptable, providing students with various ways to process their grief journey.

The group design allows students to work through common grief roadblocks, increase connection through shared experiences, and enhance their ability to cope. The American School Counselor Association (ASCA®)-aligned curriculum contains an introductory lesson, ten grief lessons, and a final closing lesson. If they have extra time, facilitators can include the initial and final lessons in the core sessions.

You'll find a range of essential resources in the book's concluding pages. These consist of permission and completion letters, attendance logs, a group expectation form, and a Certificate of Completion. You'll also find pre- and post-group surveys to measure the success of programming and templates to share the results with interested parties. Moreover, this workbook provides a comprehensive small-group action plan that will integrate effortlessly into your ASCA® evaluation document and facilitate a seamless transition from planning to assessment.

Practical and applicable, the activities provided are suitable for small- and large-group instruction and require no additional materials. You do not need to bring supplies beyond pencils, markers or crayons, and paper; you won't need to spend hours prepping materials before meeting with your students. Everything you need is included!

See page 70 for information on Downloadable Resources.

What's Included?

This **Grief Small-Group Curriculum** offers a comprehensive ten-lesson program and accompanying materials for facilitating group sessions. Following each detailed lesson outline, you'll find practical resources for establishing a small group within your school environment.

Mind Map: Provides an illustrated diagram of the grief concept being reviewed in the day's session. Students should begin each lesson by considering the meaning of the specific grief concept. It is optional to write these, but visuals are helpful for many students. Some have found it helpful to draw the Mind Map on the board, or you can draw a tree with the grief concept written on the trunk and the related words on the fruit of the tree.

ASCA® Standards: Each lesson includes success criteria for the learning target.

Lesson Introduction: At the start of each lesson, we will introduce a concept and explain it to provide clarity for the upcoming story.

Circle Time Questions: This section has three optional questions for the facilitator to start the conversation. These questions allow students to deepen their understanding of the topic and build community by discussing and sharing their experiences.

Story Time: Provides stories related to the concept that should be read aloud to help children understand the concept.

Discussion Questions: Students can discuss the questions posed to help them process their beliefs on the subject.

Processing Activities: Including round robin discussion, these activities offer opportunities to reflect and process their loss in a supportive group setting.

Additional Activities: Provides extra activities to help students reflect and process their loss.

Closing Considerations: Is an opportunity to review the concept and ask students to reflect on their new experience with the material.

Grief Connection Cards: Provide an opportunity for meaningful and lively group interaction related to the lesson topics.

Accompanying Group Documents

Small Group Action Plan Guide: Provides the necessary information required to complete the ASCA® National Model's Small Group Action Plan.

Permission Form: The permission form is used to gain the permission of the student's caregivers for the child to attend the Grief group. Be sure to send this home about two weeks before the group starts.

Group Expectations: These provide basic expectations for the group process. The form has space for the facilitator and group to collaborate on adding additional expectations to fit their group.

Group Attendance Form: This is a blank form that allows the facilitator to track which students attended each session and what topics were discussed.

Group Attendance Form (Example): This form is an example of how to best utilize the group attendance form.

Pre- and Post-Group Survey: Provides an opportunity for students to share what they know of the concepts before and after they've completed the curriculum.

To measure the progress of students who participate, use the same assessment for both the pre-group and post-group survey. Administer the pre-group survey at the start of the instructional period, followed by instruction and practice opportunities for measured skills or knowledge.

Group Attendance Form

At the end of the instructional period, administer the post-survey and compare the results of both surveys to identify areas of improvement and areas that need further instruction. Then calculate the average score of the pre-survey and post-survey and determine the percentage of improvement by subtracting the pre-survey average from the post-survey average and then dividing the result by the pre-survey average. Use this pre-survey average improvement to measure the students' progress effectively.

Percentage of Improvement Formula:
(Post-Group Total - Pre-Group Total / Pre-Group Total) x 100 = Percentage of Overall Improvement

Example:
(44 Post-Group Total - 31 Pre-Group Total / 31) x 100 = 41.94% Overall Improvement

Look at your data to determine who should attend your group. Review recent losses in your community, attendance data, conduct referrals, and achievement metrics and look for students with deficits. Children are typically ready to begin processing their grief 3-6 months following a loss, however this is dependent on the child. Some children benefit from earlier intervention, while others need more time before they are ready to participate in supportive services. Consider also tracking your students' academic achievements, absences, and discipline referrals. You can better see the impact of your small groups when strategically selecting students and closely monitoring their academic, attendance, and conduct metrics. Be sure to share the results of your intervention with your advisory council.

Post-Group Survey Results: The survey shows one way to share your data with your interested parties. Remember, we want to make sure that we use graphs and charts as they show our data, which is often more impactful than a paragraph of text. Use whatever platform you prefer to show your data but be sure to complete the data following the group and then share with your interested parties.

Post-Group Survey Results (Example): The survey shows what your data might resemble following the completion of the groups. You can use this form to share your data.

Certificate of Completion: Present students with a certificate to congratulate them on completing the curriculum.

Grief Group Completion Letter: Letter written to the caregivers/guardians of students following the completion of the group. Provide students with their certificate and their group review letter during the last session.

A **Coping Skill List** provides students with various coping strategies to try during difficult times.

Additional Materials: We promised to provide everything you need in this workbook, and we have. However, you will need to make copies of the pre- and post-group assessment surveys. You might also print and cut the Grief Connection Cards to help facilitate that activity verbally. It might also be helpful to have some fidgets accessible for your students during their group session.

Good luck with your group! We hope you have a meaningful experience supporting your students with grief!

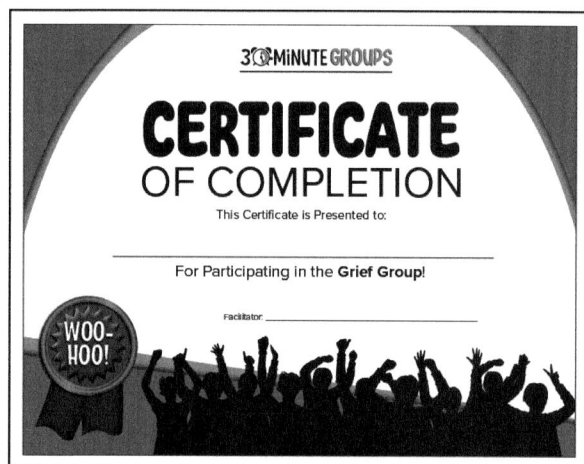

Introductory Group Session

Directions and Overview

The introductory group session is recommended; however, the content of this introductory meeting can easily be integrated into the first grief session, My Grief is Unique, if preferred.

Directions: At the first meeting with the group, introduce yourself and warmly welcome everyone. Explain the purpose of the group and encourage the students, acknowledging that while discussing grief can be challenging, they will all grow together and even find moments of fun along the way.

Survey: Share with the group that the first thing they are going to complete is the pre-group survey. Encourage students to complete the survey honestly and remind them there are no right or wrong answers. Once students have completed the survey, have them turn them in to you and ensure all questions have been answered.

Introductions: Help students become more comfortable with each other by asking each one to share their name, a favorite food, and one thing they hope to get from participating in the group. Explain that during each session, they will begin the group by sharing a rose (highlight), a thorn (lowlight), and a bud (something they are looking forward to or hoping for) or an emotion thermometer where they rate their feelings on a scale of 1 (very low) to 10 (feeling awesome). Offer to practice that check-in now.

Explain the Group Format: Use this time to review with the group where, when, and how often you will meet. Share that each week, you'll be processing different aspects of grief. Explain that the group format will be a check-in, circle-time discussion, a quick story where they can color or eat (if it is a lunch bunch), and then an activity. Explain that there will be time to share and discuss as a group after each weekly activity. Finally, tell students at the end of each session that they will be asked to give a one-sentence answer concerning what they have learned or will take away from the group session.

Create Group Expectations: Print a copy of the group expectations. Review the expectations with the group and allow group members to discuss whether you need to modify or add expectations.

Group Conclusion: Ask each student to summarize the information they learned from this session into one sentence. Students can share in pairs or with the entire group.

Note to Facilitators: Sharing about and exploring grief can be challenging for all ages. Keep tissue readily available if a student has an emotional release. If you notice the group is shy or reserved, encourage students to write responses instead of sharing them aloud or have them break into pairs. If you don't have the materials on hand for a processing activity, select one of the alternate discussion-based activities. A grief group does not have to be facilitated perfectly to be effective; you simply need to create a safe and welcoming environment for all. Remember, this workbook is just the foundation—you bring it to life!

MY GRIEF IS UNIQUE

MIND MAP

On the board, draw a mind map and ask students to consider the meaning of *Grief*.

```
        SADNESS              SORROW


                    GRIEF


   HEARTBREAK                        HURT
              MOURNING
```

ASCA® STANDARDS

- **B-SMS 7.** Effective coping skills

- **B-SS 2.** Positive, respectful, and supportive relationships with students who are similar to and different from them

- **B-SS 4.** Empathy

DIRECTIONS

- Prior to the first group, ensure all students have completed the Pre-/Post-Group Survey.

- Begin the group by asking members to share a rose (highlight), a thorn (lowlight), and a bud (something they are looking forward to or hoping for). Alternatively, students can use an emotion scale where they rate their feelings on a scale of 1 (very low)–10 (feeling awesome).

- Review the Group Expectations.

- Read the Lesson Introduction and ask the Circle Time Questions before reading the Story and asking the Discussion Questions. Students can work in pairs to answer the questions or individually share with the whole group.

- Complete one of the three Process Activities. If time allows, complete the Connection Cards (in pairs or a group) and the Additional Activities.

- Be sure to complete the Closing Considerations with each lesson.

LESSON INTRODUCTION

There are many types of **loss** we may experience in life, including the death of a loved one, the death of a pet, divorce, a relationship ending, moving, or our health declining. **Grief** is the emotional response we have to a loss. Grief looks and feels differently for everyone. There is no timeline for how long someone may grieve, and everyone processes their grief in unique ways.

Ask students to reflect and share their answers to the following questions with the group.

- What are different types of losses you or someone you know might experience (a friendship ending, the death of a loved one, a parent divorce, etc.)?

- What losses do you think are the hardest to experience and why?

- How would you describe grief to a friend?

STORY TIME

Coping with Sudden Loss

Sloane and Cora were sisters and best friends. They were only eighteen months apart and did everything together. They went to the same school, shared a love for sports, and loved watching movies before bed.

One day, Sloane did not come home from volleyball practice as usual. She had wanted to stay late after practice to work on her serve with the coach. Cora wondered why Sloane still wasn't home, and then their mom and dad came into Cora's room crying. They told her they had horrible news to share, and that Sloane had been killed in a car accident on the way home. Cora did not know what to do or feel. Her ears felt numb, and she screamed, "NO! THIS CAN'T BE REAL!" She couldn't imagine life without her sister. No one in her life had ever died before, and she had so many feelings and questions that she didn't know how to process.

The day after the accident, Cora's grandmother sat down with Cora. Cora said, "Gramma, I'm feeling all these things on the inside, but I don't know what they are. I feel all mixed up and just want to throw something." Cora's grandmother told her she was feeling something called grief.

Cora said, "What is grief?" Her grandmother replied, "Grief is what a person feels after someone or something they love is gone forever." Cora asked, "Why have mom and dad been crying all day, but you've only cried once?" Cora's grandmother shared that "everyone grieves a loss in their own way. Some people may cry a lot, while others, like you and me, may feel a lot of feelings on the inside but have a harder time showing or explaining them to others." Cora's grandmother then added, "There is no right or wrong way to grieve, and even if we experience the same loss, we all may feel and express it differently."

Cora then asked, "How long will we feel this grief?" Her grandmother said, "There is no set timeline for grief. We all loved Sloane very much, so we will all grieve for a long time. The most important thing to remember is that it's okay to talk and share about how you're feeling as we go through this."

DISCUSSION QUESTIONS

- How did Cora's grandmother define what grief was?

- In what ways did Cora and her parents grieve differently?

- What did Cora's grandmother say about the timeline of grief? How did it make you feel?

- Cora had a lot of questions about grief after her loss. What questions do you have about loss or grief?

PROCESSING ACTIVITY

Group processing activities allow students to remember, reflect, and find shared experiences with peers in their loss journeys.

For this week's activity, pass out a piece of paper and coloring utensils. Ask students to **draw a picture of a person or object that represents a loss they are grieving**. Once students have completed their drawing, allow them to share their images and talk about their loss if desired. You can also have students complete this processing activity by handing out modeling clay/playdough and allowing students to create a tangible object that represents whatever loss they've experienced.

ADDITIONAL ACTIVITIES

- Have students write the name of a loved one or a word that describes their relationship with that person/place/thing down the left side of the paper vertically. Next to each letter, have students write descriptive words to memorialize their loved one using each letter of the name as the first letter.

  Example:

  Dedicated
  Adventure-loving
  Dreamer

- Divide students into pairs. Have them share the name of who they lost, their relationship to that person/place/thing, and one thing they loved most about them.

CLOSING CONSIDERATIONS

Loss is when something or someone important to you is gone, and things won't be the same as they were before. Grief is how you feel after a loss. While loss is about what is gone, grief is about how you feel because of that loss. Everyone experiences and expresses loss and grief in their own ways.

To wrap up, ask students to take a moment to reflect on what they've learned about grief or on something they will take away from this week's session. Then, have them summarize their thoughts in one sentence. They can share their sentence with a partner or with the whole group. If time permits, students can also share one thing they hope to achieve or experience in the coming week.

Copy and cut out the cards for small groups to discuss. Read the cards aloud or pass out cards to students for them read during your discussion.

MY GRIEF IS UNIQUE

My grief feels like...

When I first heard about my loss, I...

I'll never forget when...

The hardest part about my grief is...

Something I've always wondered after my loss is...

When I think about my loss, I often...

Life After Loss

MIND MAP

On the board, draw a mind map and ask students to consider the meaning of *Change*.

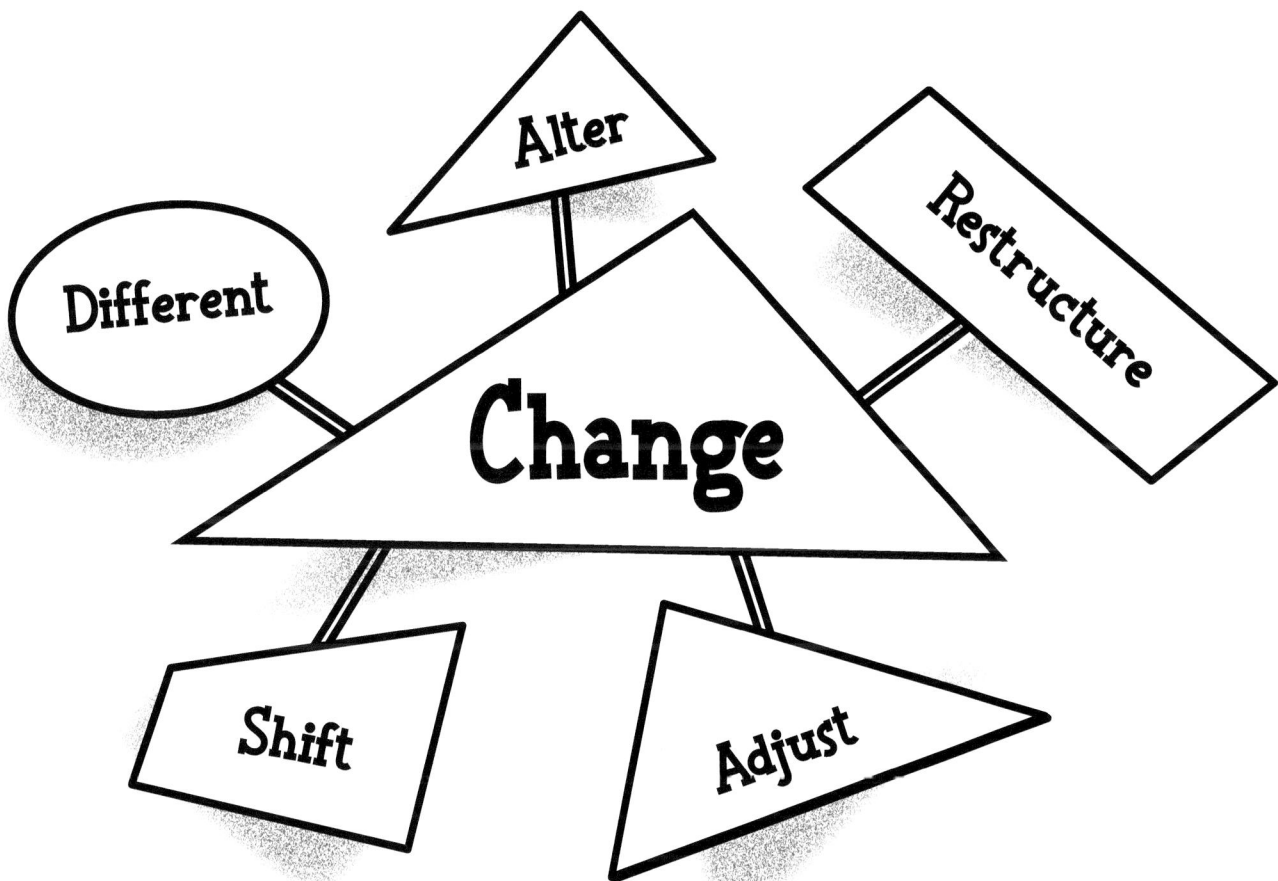

ASCA® STANDARDS

- **B-SMS 5.** Perseverance to achieve long and short-term goals
- **B-SMS 6.** Ability to identify and overcome barriers
- **B-SMS 10.** Ability to manage transitions and adapt to change

DIRECTIONS

- Begin the group by asking members to share a rose (highlight), a thorn (lowlight), and a bud (something they are looking forward to or hoping for). Alternatively, students can use an emotion scale where they rate their feelings on a scale of 1 (very low)–10 (feeling awesome).

ROSE — HIGHLIGHT | THORN — LOWLIGHT | BUD — I'M LOOKING FORWARD TO

1 2 3 4 5 6 7 8 9 10

- Review the Group Expectations.

- Read the Lesson Introduction and ask the Circle Time Questions before reading the Story and asking the Discussion Questions. Students can work in pairs to answer the questions or individually share with the whole group.

- Complete one of the three Process Activities. If time allows, complete the Connection Cards (in pairs or a group) and the Additional Activities.

- Be sure to complete the Closing Considerations with each lesson.

LESSON INTRODUCTION

A loss can bring about lots of **change**. Loss can change family dynamics, routines and habits, living conditions, relationships, and many other areas of life. Some changes may not feel big or noticeable, while other changes may feel large and extremely difficult to navigate. While we can't control many of the changes we may encounter following a loss, it can be helpful to identify areas of change and ways we can adapt to those changes.

Ask students to reflect and share their answers to the following questions with the group.

- What is one way your life has changed since your loss?

- What was an unexpected change that has affected you since your loss?

- What are some family changes you've experienced at home since your loss?

STORY TIME

Navigating Change After Divorce

Coco and Miguel had heard about divorce from their friends at school but never imagined it would happen in their own family. That changed when their dad told them he was leaving at the end of the week and moving to Mexico.

This was a total shock to both Coco and Miguel. They never saw their parents fight and didn't understand why their dad would want to move so far away without them. When they asked their dad, "Why?" He responded quickly, "I just have to go. I'm not sure if or when I will be back."

Life changed quickly for Coco and Miguel. They went from living with both parents to only having their mom at home. Their mom now had to work two jobs to support the family, often leaving them in the care of their aunt. They also had to move to a small apartment farther away from their school and friends. Frustrated, both kept saying, "This isn't fair!" Their mom responded, "It is what it is, and we just have to move forward."

Despite the challenges and confusion at home, Coco and Miguel looked forward to going to school every day, where they still had the same teachers, friends, and routines. One day at lunch, their friend Kelley, who used to live in their old neighborhood, asked how they were adjusting to the new apartment. Both made angry faces, showing their disapproval. Kelley then suggested they have a playdate that weekend. Coco hesitated at first, feeling embarrassed about her dad leaving them, but then she remembered their new apartment complex had a pool. She invited Kelley to come swim, and they all got excited about the upcoming fun. Although most of the changes at home were hard, Coco and Miguel also found some positives in their situation with the help of friends and family.

DISCUSSION QUESTIONS

- What types of loss did Coco and Miguel experience?

- In what ways did Coco and Miguel's lives change after their dad left the country?

- Coco and Miguel often said, "This isn't fair." What do you think they meant by this?

- How did Coco and Miguel adapt to their changes?

PROCESSING ACTIVITY

Group processing activities allow students to remember, reflect, and find shared experiences with peers in their loss journeys.

For this week's activity, pass out a piece of paper and have students fold the paper in half. Have students label one half **"Before Loss"** and the other half **"After Loss"** and then encourage students to reflect and draw what life looked like for them before their loss and after their loss. Once complete, ask students to share what changes they've noticed in their lives and how they feel about those changes.

ADDITIONAL ACTIVITIES

- Have students partner up and share three to five ways their lives have changed since their loss. For each change identified, have students name at least one emotion they've felt about that specific change.

- Pass out a piece of paper and have students draw a large circle and a smaller one within the big circle. Have students label the outside circle as "Outside of my control" and the smaller circle as "Inside my control." Have students write things about their loss that are outside of their control (for example: New home, my future, dad crying all the time, etc.) and then have them write things they are still in control of (for example: my thoughts, getting rest, talking about my feelings, etc.). Share with the group that spending more time focused on what we can control versus what we can't control, even when dealing with loss is helpful.

CLOSING CONSIDERATIONS

Change often follows a loss. Some changes may affect you daily, while others may hardly be noticeable. Sticking to a routine, focusing on the things within your control, and asking for help as needed can help you navigate change after a loss.

To wrap up, ask students to take a moment to reflect on what they've learned about grief or something they will take away from this week's session. Then, have them summarize their thoughts in one sentence. They can share their sentence with a partner or with the whole group. If time permits, students can also share one thing they hope to achieve or experience in the coming week.

Copy and cut out the cards for small groups to discuss. Read the cards aloud or pass out cards to students for them read during your discussion.

Life After Loss

Since my loss,
my family has...

The biggest change
I've noticed since
my loss is...

One relationship
that has changed
since my loss is...

One new habit
I've started since
my loss is...

One thing I've noticed
about my physical health
since my loss is...

One goal or priority
I've made since
my loss is...

MIXED BAG OF GRIEF

MIND MAP

On the board, draw a mind map and ask students to consider the meaning of *Feelings*.

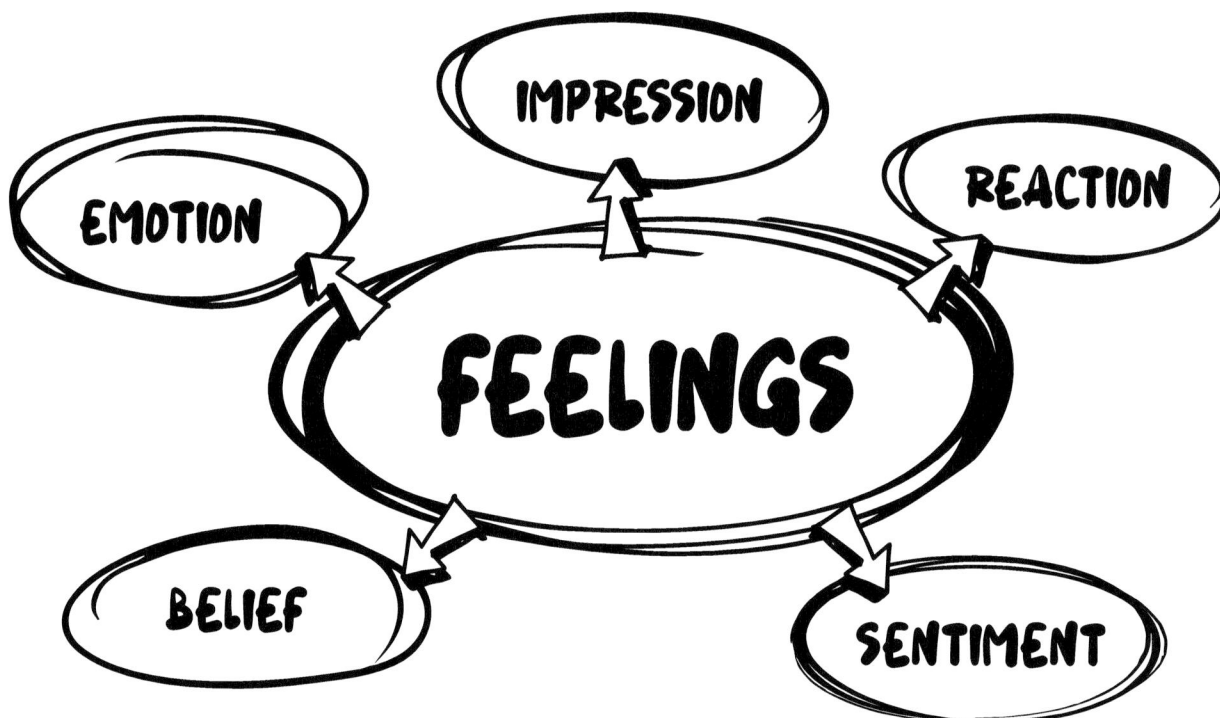

IMPRESSION

EMOTION

REACTION

FEELINGS

BELIEF

SENTIMENT

ASCA® STANDARDS

- **B-SMS 6.** Ability to identify and overcome barriers

- **B-SMS 7.** Effective coping skills

- **B-SS 1.** Effective oral and written communication skills and listening skills

- Begin the group by asking members to share a rose (highlight), a thorn (lowlight), and a bud (something they are looking forward to or hoping for). Alternatively, students can use an emotion scale where they rate their feelings on a scale of 1 (very low)–10 (feeling awesome).

ROSE
HIGHLIGHT

THORN
LOWLIGHT

BUD
I'M LOOKING
FORWARD TO

1 2 3 4 5 6 7 8 9 10

- Review the Group Expectations.

- Read the Lesson Introduction and ask the Circle Time Questions before reading the Story and asking the Discussion Questions. Students can work in pairs to answer the questions or individually share with the whole group.

- Complete one of the three Process Activities. If time allows, complete the Connection Cards (in pairs or a group) and the Additional Activities.

- Be sure to complete the Closing Considerations with each lesson.

LESSON INTRODUCTION

When we experience a loss, we often experience a variety of **feelings.** Some of the most common feelings individuals experience after a loss are sadness, anger, denial, guilt, worry, and sometimes even relief. At times, the feelings we experience in grief feel big and messy, while other times, they feel small and controlled. Having a wide range of feelings is normal and acceptable. These feelings can affect our thoughts, bodies, and behaviors. It is important to reflect and share how we are feeling throughout the grieving process. There are no right or wrong feelings in grief, and no one should feel like they need to hide from or hold in their feelings.

Ask students to reflect and share their answers to the following questions with the group.

- What feelings have you experienced the most since your loss?

- Where in your body do you feel your emotions?

- What feeling has been the most difficult to manage since your loss?

STORY TIME

Learning to Miss Wrigley

Carter had loved animals since he was a little boy, and as soon as he could talk, he began asking his parents for a dog. On his fifth birthday, Carter's wish came true when his parents got him a dog named Wrigley. The two quickly became inseparable. Wrigley slept in Carter's room, attended all his baseball games, and played fetch with him every night.

Wrigley was always there to cheer Carter up after a tough day at school or calm his nerves before a big test. As time passed, both Carter and Wrigley grew older. Wrigley slowed down, and one day, he stopped eating. When Carter got home from school one afternoon, his mom told him they needed to take Wrigley to the vet. The vet delivered heartbreaking news: Wrigley had cancer and only had a few months left to live.

Carter was devastated but made the most of their remaining time together. He gave Wrigley extra treats and tummy rubs, cherishing every moment. One day, Wrigley wouldn't get out of bed, and Carter knew it was time to say goodbye. At the vet, Carter gave Wrigley one last hug.

In the hours and days after Wrigley died, Carter felt a lot of things. He felt very sad— especially when Wrigley did not greet him at the door. The first night without Wrigley curled up next to his bed, Carter couldn't fall asleep.

Carter was also angry: He didn't understand why such a good dog had to die. His anger made him yell at his parents when they asked him to do chores.

Along with his sadness and anger, Carter also felt relieved. He was glad Wrigley was no longer sick and in pain. And he felt joy remembering all the special days he had with Wrigley, especially those nights in the backyard playing fetch. Although Wrigley was no longer with him, he knew he would remember their special bond for the rest of his life.

DISCUSSION QUESTIONS

- What were some of the different emotions Carter felt throughout his story?
- How do you think Carter's feelings may have affected his behavior or physical body?
- What are some healthy ways Carter could express his feelings of sadness and anger?
- What does Carter's story teach us about feelings and grief?

PROCESSING ACTIVITY

Group processing activities allow students to remember, reflect, and find shared experiences with peers in their loss journeys.

For this week's activity, pass out a piece of paper and coloring utensils. Ask students to trace one of their own feet with a marker. Then have students write feeling words and draw pictures within their footprint that represent how they have felt since their loss. After all students are finished, ask students to complete the sentence: "**Walking in my grief shoes feels like**
_____."

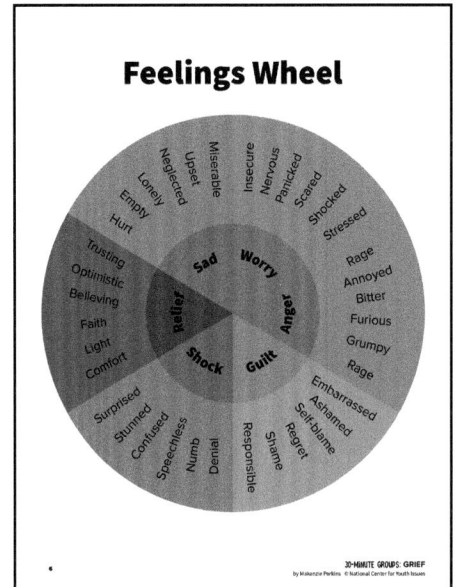

Feelings Wheel

ADDITIONAL ACTIVITIES

- Have students write a letter to their loved one. In the letter, encourage them to talk about how they have been feeling, what they miss the most about their loved one, and their favorite memory.

- Have students think about a specific feeling they've experienced related to their grief. It could be a recent feeling or one that has been significant for them all along. Divide the group into pairs, and have the students share with their partners what emotion they thought of and why.

CLOSING CONSIDERATIONS

After a loss, it is normal to feel a lot of different emotions. Your feelings may change a lot and can vary in intensity. Talking about your feelings with someone you trust can help you understand and manage them as you grieve.

To wrap up, ask students to take a moment to reflect on what they've learned about grief or something they will take away from this week's session. Then, have them summarize their thoughts in one sentence. They can share their sentence with a partner or with the whole group. If time permits, each student can also share one thing they hope to achieve or experience in the coming week.

Copy and cut out the cards for small groups to discuss. Read the cards aloud or pass out cards to students for them read during your discussion.

MIXED BAG OF GRIEF

The most surprising thing I've noticed about grief is...

A way I express my grief is through...

When I feel sad about their absence, I...

One emotion I struggle with is...

I feel comforted when...

A feeling I wish I could understand better is...

Grief Bursts

MIND MAP

On the board, draw a mind map and ask students to consider the meaning of *Grief Burst*.

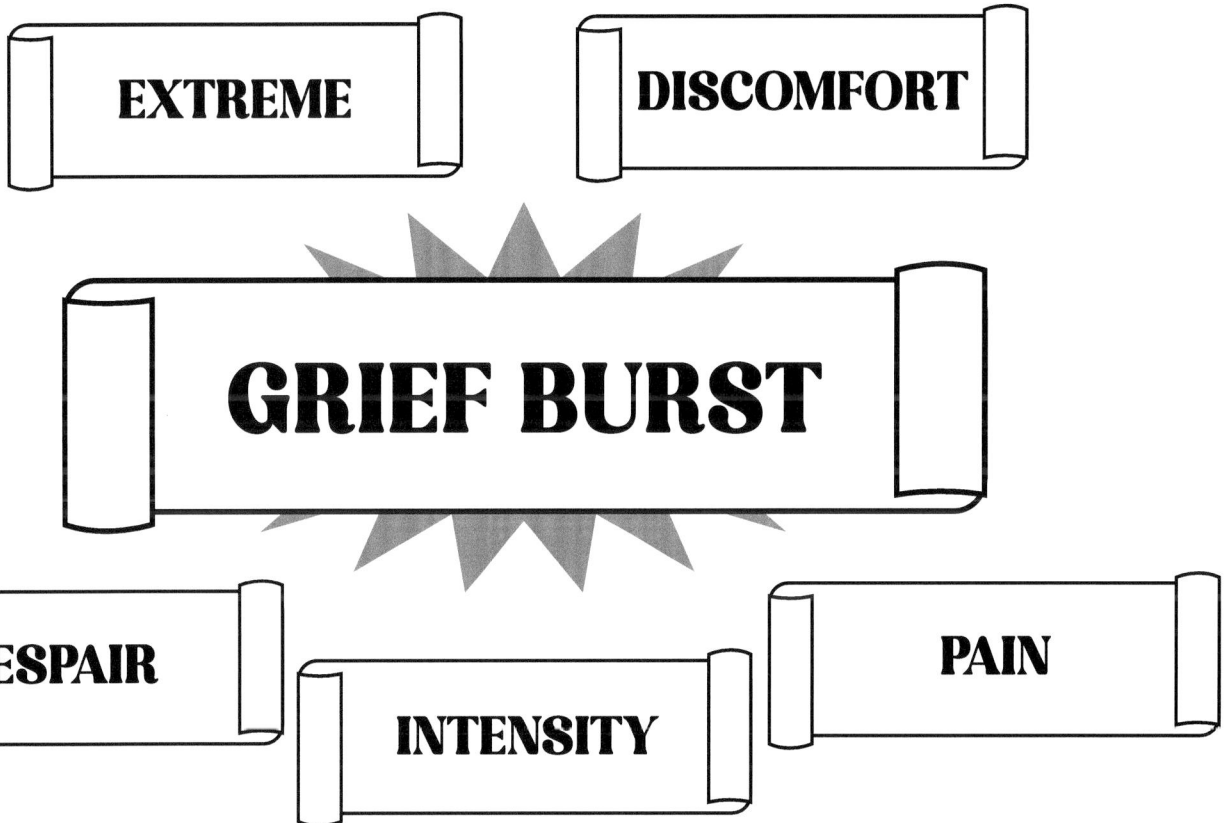

EXTREME

DISCOMFORT

GRIEF BURST

DESPAIR

INTENSITY

PAIN

ASCA® STANDARDS

- **B-SMS 1.** Responsibility for self and actions
- **B-SMS 6.** Ability to identify and overcome barriers
- **B-SMS 10.** Ability to manage transitions and adapt to change

DIRECTIONS

- Begin the group by asking members to share a rose (highlight), a thorn (lowlight), and a bud (something they are looking forward to or hoping for). Alternatively, students can use an emotion scale where they rate their feelings on a scale of 1 (very low)–10 (feeling awesome).

- Review the Group Expectations.

- Read the Lesson Introduction and ask the Circle Time Questions before reading the Story and asking the Discussion Questions. Students can work in pairs to answer the questions or individually share with the whole group.

- Complete one of the three Process Activities. If time allows, complete the Connection Cards (in pairs or a group) and the Additional Activities.

- Be sure to complete the Closing Considerations with each lesson.

LESSON INTRODUCTION

A **grief burst** is a sudden wave of intense feelings that can happen at any time following a loss. Grief bursts often occur out of the blue, triggered by a random memory, smell, song, or photograph. Other times, grief bursts can be anticipated, like on an anniversary, holiday, or birthday. Grief bursts can feel overwhelming in the moment, but just like a thunderstorm comes and goes, these bursts of feelings don't last forever either.

CIRCLE TIME QUESTIONS

Ask students to reflect and share their answers to the following questions with the group.

- What are some things that may remind you of your loss?

- How might you notice if a grief burst is coming?

- Have you ever experienced a grief burst? What was it like for you?

STORY TIME

Mimi's Favorite Song

Rome and Zuri lived in a quiet neighborhood with their mom and dad. Their grandma, whom they called Mimi, used to live with them, too. A few months ago, Mimi went to the hospital, where her heart stopped beating, and she died. Rome and Zuri's parents explained this was because when Mimi's heart stopped beating, all the other important parts of her body couldn't work anymore either.

Ever since, Rome and Zuri have experienced a lot of different feelings. Rome feels a lot of sadness as he misses spending time with his Mimi. Zuri feels a lot of anger and spends a lot of time wishing the doctors could fix Mimi's heart.

One day, Rome and Zuri went to a coffee shop with their mom. Right after ordering a special pastry, Zuri started crying. Zuri's mom asked, "What is wrong, Zuri?" Zuri replied, "Do you hear that? Mimi's favorite song is playing. I miss her so much! I want to go home right now!"

DISCUSSION QUESTIONS

- What triggered Zuri's grief burst at the coffee shop?

- Why do you think Zuri reacted the way she did when she heard Mimi's favorite song?

- Why is it important to allow ourselves to feel or express our emotions when grieving or having a grief burst?

- What are some ways Rome or Zuri's mom can help support Zuri when she gets upset about missing Mimi?

PROCESSING ACTIVITY

Group processing activities allow students to remember, reflect, and find shared experiences with peers in their loss journeys.

For this week's activity, ask group members to fill out the **My Grief Volcano Worksheet**. Once completed, group members can share their triggers with others and discuss ways they can safely help tame their volcanoes so they don't explode.

My Grief Volcano Worksheet

Level 1:
Things that don't bother me

Level 2:
Things that make me uncomfortable

Level 3:
Things that upset me

Level 4:
Things that make me feel overwhelmed

Level 5:
Things that make me explode with feelings

⑤

④

❸

❷

❶

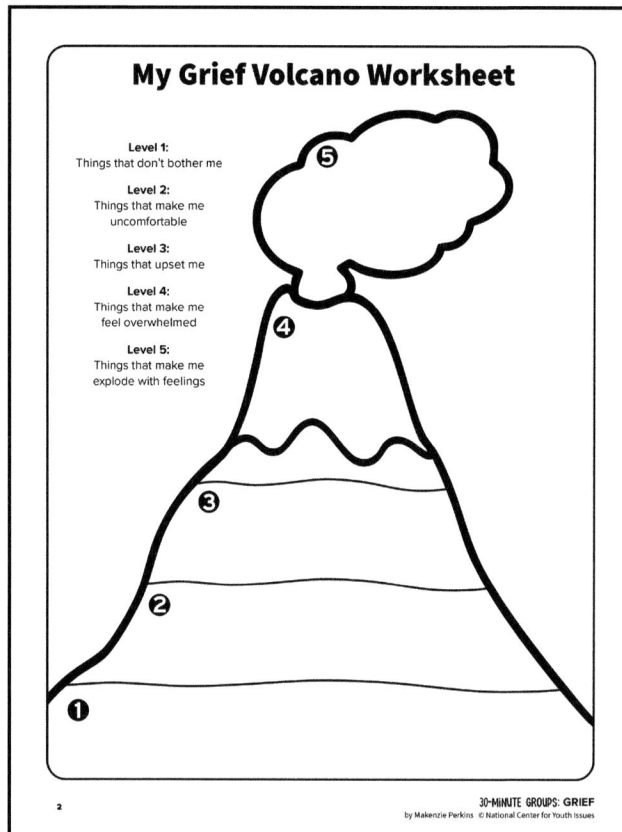

ADDITIONAL ACTIVITIES

- Allow students to partner up and share a time they have experienced a grief burst. Encourage students to share what they think triggered the grief burst, how it felt in the moment, and what helped them feel better afterward.

- Pass out a piece of paper and a writing utensil. Ask students to write down or draw places, objects, or events that may trigger big feelings related to their loss. Allow students to share these with a partner or a group. Then, ask students to brainstorm together how they may safely manage a grief burst.

CLOSING CONSIDERATIONS

A grief burst happens when you suddenly feel strong emotions about your loss. It is a normal part of grieving, even long after a loss has occurred. Acknowledging your feelings, finding a safe space, and talking to a trusted support person can help you manage the intense emotions that often come with a grief burst.

To wrap up, ask students to take a moment to reflect on what they've learned about grief or something they will take away from this week's session. Then, have them summarize their thoughts in one sentence. They can share their sentence with a partner or with the whole group. If time permits, each student can also share one thing they hope to achieve or experience in the coming week.

Copy and cut out the cards for small groups to discuss. Read the cards aloud or pass out cards to students for them read during your discussion.

Grief Bursts

When I feel
a grief burst
coming on, I....

A common
trigger for my
grief bursts is...

One feeling
I struggle to
manage is....

During a
grief burst,
I usually....

Someone who
I find supportive in
my grief journey is...

The thing that
usually calms me down
during a grief burst is...

WAYS TO REMEMBER

MIND MAP

On the board, draw a mind map and ask students to consider the meaning of *Memories*.

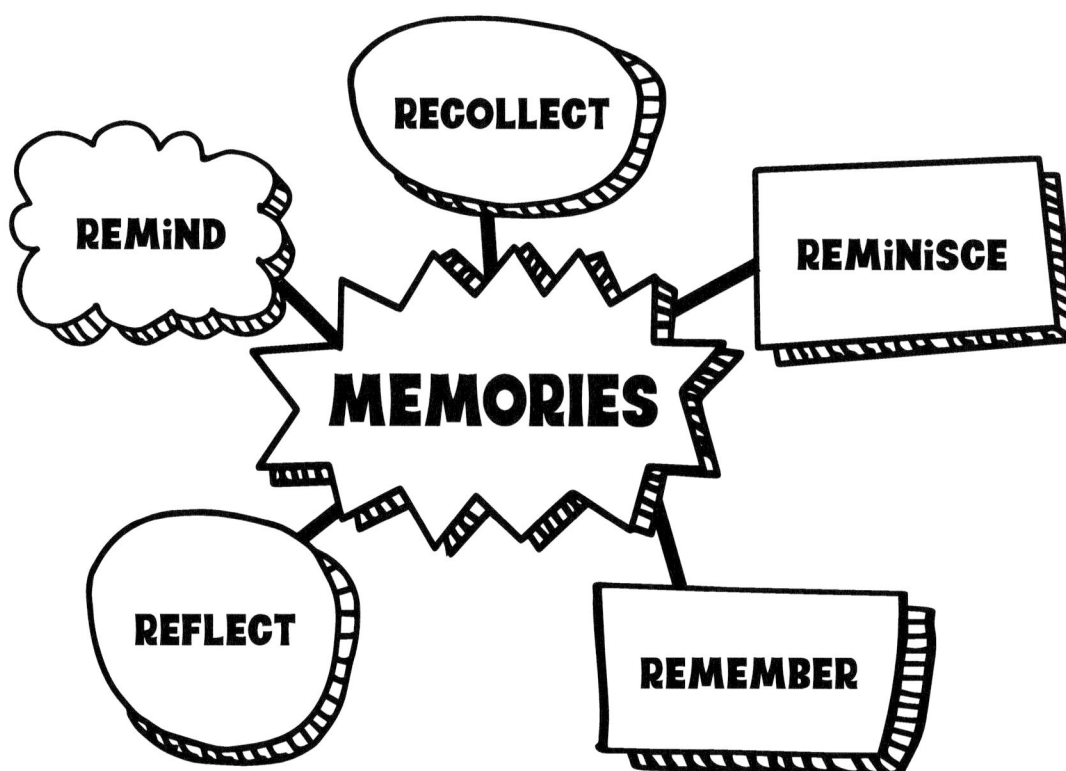

ASCA® STANDARDS

- **B-SS 2.** Positive, respectful, and supportive relationships with students who are similar to and different from them

- **B-SMS 6.** Ability to identify and overcome barriers

- **B-SMS 7.** Effective coping skills

- Begin the group by asking members to share a rose (highlight), a thorn (lowlight), and a bud (something they are looking forward to or hoping for). Alternatively, students can use an emotion scale where they rate their feelings on a scale of 1 (very low)–10 (feeling awesome).

ROSE — HIGHLIGHT | THORN — LOWLIGHT | BUD — I'M LOOKING FORWARD TO

1 2 3 4 5 6 7 8 9 10

- Review the Group Expectations.

- Read the Lesson Introduction and ask the Circle Time Questions before reading the Story and asking the Discussion Questions. Students can work in pairs to answer the questions or individually share with the whole group.

- Complete one of the three Process Activities. If time allows, complete the Connection Cards (in pairs or a group) and the Additional Activities.

- Be sure to complete the Closing Considerations with each lesson.

LESSON INTRODUCTION

To **remember** means to keep something safe in our minds. We remember special times and memories with people we love even after they have died. While preserving and sharing these memories can sometimes bring comfort, it can also feel difficult or sad, and that is okay. We may not always remember all our special memories, and that is okay, too. There are many ways to remember our loved ones. We can talk about memories, reflect quietly, create art that symbolizes our loved ones, look at photos, listen to meaningful music, or even participate in a grief ritual.

Ask students to reflect and share their answers to the following questions with the group.

- How do you like to remember your loved one?

- What is one of your favorite memories of the person/thing you have lost?

- When is a time you saw, heard, touched, or smelled something that reminded you of your loved one?

STORY TIME

A Flower for Mom

Olivia, Zach, Maddie, and Bryan always played together at recess. Their favorite game was tag, and they would start chasing each other around the playground as soon as they got outside after lunch. Most days, their teacher, Mrs. Drake, had to remind them not to run in the hallways until they were outside.

One sunny spring day, Zach told the group he didn't want to play. He went to sit on the bench and curled into a ball, staring at his feet. Olivia, Maddie, and Bryan were confused because Zach always loved playing tag. Olivia decided to go talk to Zach on the bench.

She asked him, "Are you okay, buddy?" Zach responded, "I'm having a horrible day because I miss my mom." Olivia knew Zach's mom had died a few years ago after a long battle with cancer. She replied, "I'm here for you if you want to talk about your mom, or I can just sit here with you if you'd like." Zach said, "The warm sun reminds me of when my mom, sister, and I would go to the beach and play for hours. I miss those days, and I miss our beach picnics."

Olivia said, "Those sound like some fun, special memories. I'm sorry your mom isn't here anymore." Zach thanked her for listening and said, "Sometimes it just helps to talk about my favorite times with my mom when I'm missing her."

Zach then got up from the bench, walked over to a blooming bush, and picked a pink flower. Pink was his mom's favorite color. He looked at the flower, took a moment to remember his mom's warm hugs, then tucked the flower in his pocket, ran over to his friends, and said, "I'm ready to play tag now!" And off they went.

DISCUSSION QUESTIONS

- What might Zach have been feeling when he went over to the bench?

- How did Olivia help support her friend Zach?

- What are some of the ways Zach decided to remember his mom at recess?

- What do you think Zach was thinking about when he picked the pink flower and put it in his pocket?

PROCESSING ACTIVITY

Group processing activities allow students to remember, reflect, and find shared experiences with peers in their loss journeys.

For this week's activity, pass out a piece of paper and coloring supplies. Ask students to quietly reflect and remember some of their favorite memories of the person or thing they are grieving. Then, ask them to **draw a picture of that memory** on the paper. Once complete, allow students to share their special memory with the group.

ADDITIONAL ACTIVITIES

- Provide students with magazines, scissors, and paper. Have them cut and paste pictures and words that represent memories of their loved ones. Allow students to share their memory collages with the group.

- Have students partner up in pairs of two. Give each student about five minutes to share a special memory (or memories) of their loved one they never want to forget. Once each partner gets a chance to share, come back together as a group and allow members to share special memories with the entire group.

CLOSING CONSIDERATIONS

Remembering is recalling special memories, moments, and experiences. It helps us stay connected to the people and things we've lost. While remembering can bring joy to our grief, it can also be challenging. As time goes on, it might get harder to recall certain memories, details, or feelings. However, not being able to remember something doesn't mean you love your special person any less; it's simply a natural part of the grieving process.

To wrap up, ask students to take a moment to reflect on what they've learned about remembering their loved one or something they will take away from this week's session. Then, have them summarize their thoughts in one sentence. They can share their sentence with a partner or with the whole group. If time permits, each student can also share one thing they hope to achieve or experience in the coming week.

Copy and cut out the cards for small groups to discuss. Read the cards aloud or pass out cards to students for them read during your discussion.

WAYS TO REMEMBER

I feel closest to my loved one when...

My favorite memory of who/what I've lost is...

One way I keep their memory alive is by...

A song that reminds me of them is...

A place that feels special because of them is...

When I look at their picture, I feel...

Naming and Taming the Worries

MIND MAP

On the board, draw a mind map and ask students to consider the meaning of *Worry*.

ANXIOUS

CONCERN

PANIC

WORRY

DWELL

NERVOUS

ASCA® STANDARDS

- **B-SMS 1.** Responsibility for self and actions
- **B-SMS 2.** Self-discipline and self-control
- **B-SMS 6.** Ability to identify and overcome barriers
- **B-SS 4.** Empathy

- Begin the group by asking members to share a rose (highlight), a thorn (lowlight), and a bud (something they are looking forward to or hoping for). Alternatively, students can use an emotion scale where they rate their feelings on a scale of 1 (very low)–10 (feeling awesome).

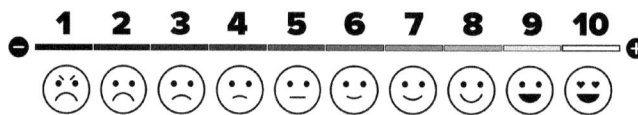

ROSE — HIGHLIGHT | THORN — LOWLIGHT | BUD — I'M LOOKING FORWARD TO

1 2 3 4 5 6 7 8 9 10

- Review the Group Expectations.

- Read the Lesson Introduction and ask the Circle Time Questions before reading the Story and asking the Discussion Questions. Students can work in pairs to answer the questions or individually share with the whole group.

- Complete one of the three Process Activities. If time allows, complete the Connection Cards (in pairs or a group) and the Additional Activities.

- Be sure to complete the Closing Considerations with each lesson.

LESSON INTRODUCTION

Worries are thoughts that pop into our heads that can make us feel concerned, unsafe, or insecure. Everyone has worries, especially when we lose something we love. When grieving, you may worry about what may happen: death, your loved ones, other people's reactions, or even forgetting memories. Sometimes, worry can make you feel tearful, tingly in your stomach, keep you up at night, or come in your dreams. Talking to someone you trust can help prevent your worries from getting stuck.

Ask students to reflect and share their answers to the following questions with the group.

- What is a worry you've had since you experienced your loss?

- When you've experienced a worry in the past, what was it like for you?

- Do your worries change or feel different when you're in different places? How so?

STORY TIME

Mia's Big Worries

Mia was a lively and excited child who could often be found dancing and singing throughout her day. But recently, something had changed.

Mia had lost her cherished aunt, who would always bake delicious desserts with her and share incredible stories and photos from her travels around the world. Since her aunt died, Mia found it hard to dance, sing, or enjoy any of her favorite activities.

One sunny Saturday, Mia sat eating breakfast at the table quietly with a worried look on her face. Her dad noticed how worried she looked and gently asked, "Mia, what is on your mind?"

Mia took a deep breath. "I just really miss Aunt Hannah, and I have this terrible fear that something bad will happen to you or Mom! And I am so afraid I will forget the sound of her voice or the smell of her amazing chocolate cake baking in her kitchen. I never want to forget those things."

Mia's dad nodded, understanding how she felt. "It is normal to feel worries like this after a loss," he said. He reached across the table and took her hand. "Your mom and I are healthy and safe right now. If something were ever to happen to both of us, your Uncle Robbie would take fantastic care of you. Instead of focusing on what might happen, I think we should bake Aunt Hannah's famous chocolate cake and share our favorite stories of her. Are you in?"

Mia exclaimed, "Let's do it!" They spent the day in the kitchen, mixing ingredients and laughing as they recounted funny stories about Aunt Hannah's adventures. Mia noticed she felt a lot better when she shared her worries out loud. She also realized that even though she missed her aunt, the memories they created together would always be a part of her.

DISCUSSION QUESTIONS

- What were some of Mia's worries after her loss?

- How did baking the chocolate cake help Mia with her worries?

- What do you think Mia learned about worries by the end of the story?

- What do you think would have happened if Mia had kept her worries to herself instead of sharing them?

PROCESSING ACTIVITY

Group processing activities allow students to remember, reflect, and find shared experiences with peers in their loss journeys.

Have students form a circle and take turns **sharing a worry they've experienced** after their loss. After everyone has had the opportunity to share, invite group members to offer helpful tips or strategies they've used to manage or ease their worries.

ADDITIONAL ACTIVITIES

- Pass out paper and coloring utensils. Ask students to design a worry monster—encourage them to create any type of monster they want. Once students have drawn their worry monsters, tell them to always keep the monster with them. If they begin having a worry, encourage them to feed the worry to their worry monster so they no longer have to carry it in their mind and body.

- Pass out white pieces of notebook paper and writing utensils. Have students write down any worries they've had since their loss. Give students a few minutes to share these worries with each other. Then instruct students to crumple their papers into "snowballs," then allow them to have a one-minute "snowball fight." Encourage students to imagine letting go of their worries as they throw their snowballs across the room.

CLOSING CONSIDERATIONS

When something scary or sad happens, such as a loss, it can bring on worries. When we hold onto worries by ourselves, they can start to affect our thoughts, behaviors, and moods. Sharing our worries helps us understand them better and keep them under control.

To wrap up, ask students to take a moment to reflect on what they've learned about grief or something they will take away from this week's session. Then, have them summarize their thoughts in one sentence. They can share their sentence with a partner or with the whole group. If time permits, each student can also share one thing they hope to achieve or experience in the coming week.

Copy and cut out the cards for small groups to discuss. Read the cards aloud or pass out cards to students for them read during your discussion.

Naming and Taming the Worries

One thing I find myself worrying about often is...

A place I usually worry more than others is...

When I start to feel worried, I...

Someone who helps me when I'm worried is...

When I worry, my body feels like...

Something I want others to know when I'm worried is...

GRiEF SPEAK: HANDLiNG DiFFiCULT CONVERSATiONS

MIND MAP

On the board, draw a mind map and ask students to consider the meaning of *Difficult Conversations*.

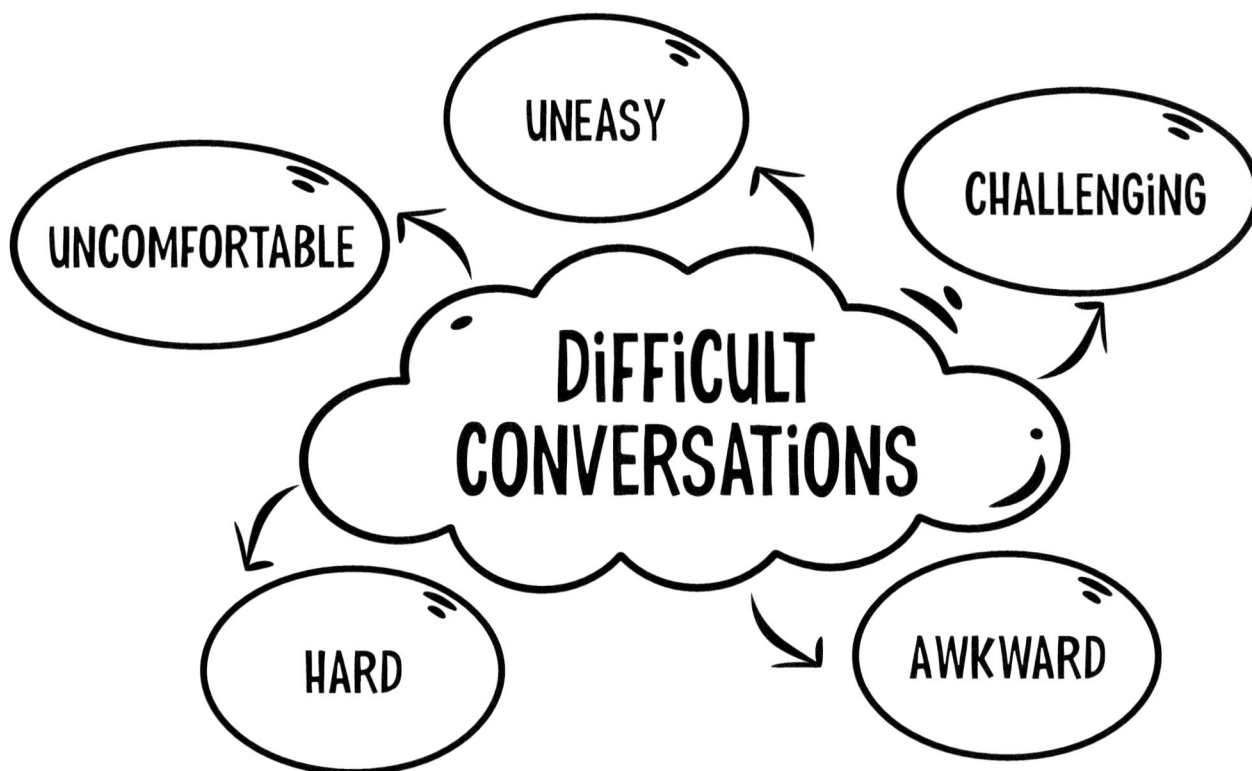

UNEASY

UNCOMFORTABLE

CHALLENGiNG

DiFFiCULT CONVERSATiONS

HARD

AWKWARD

ASCA® STANDARDS

- **B-SMS 1.** Responsibility for self and actions

- **B-SMS 2.** Self-discipline and self-control

- **B-SS 2.** Positive, respectful, and supportive relationships with students who are similar to and different from them

- **B-SS 4.** Empathy

- Begin the group by asking members to share a rose (highlight), a thorn (lowlight), and a bud (something they are looking forward to or hoping for). Alternatively, students can use an emotion scale where they rate their feelings on a scale of 1 (very low)–10 (feeling awesome).

ROSE
HIGHLIGHT

THORN
LOWLIGHT

BUD
I'M LOOKING
FORWARD TO

1 2 3 4 5 6 7 8 9 10

- Review the Group Expectations.

- Read the Lesson Introduction and ask the Circle Time Questions before reading the Story and asking the Discussion Questions. Students can work in pairs to answer the questions or individually share with the whole group.

- Complete one of the three Process Activities. If time allows, complete the Connection Cards (in pairs or a group) and the Additional Activities.

- Be sure to complete the Closing Considerations with each lesson.

LESSON INTRODUCTION

We all respond uniquely to different situations, including loss. After a loss, some classmates and adults may not know what to say or how to act toward someone who is grieving. This can sometimes result in hurtful or unhelpful words and actions that make our loss feel even more difficult to manage. It is important to **communicate our feelings** throughout the grief process so others have a better understanding of how we are doing and what needs we have.

CIRCLE TIME QUESTIONS

Ask students to reflect and share their answers to the following questions with the group.

- What is something someone has said or done that has been *helpful* during your grief journey?

- What is something someone has said or done that has been *hurtful* during your grief journey?

- What do you wish your teachers or classmates knew about your loss or grief?

STORY TIME

Finding Comfort in Connection

Memphis was nervous to come back to school. Everyone in his class knew his dad was in a car accident last week and did not survive his injuries. He was worried people would treat him differently or make fun of him if he started crying or had an emotional outburst.

With his mom's encouragement, Memphis returned to school. As soon as Memphis walked into the classroom, he noticed that the room got very quiet. Several classmates looked at him, but no one said anything directly to him. This hurt Memphis's feelings, and he started crying.

Memphis's teacher walked with him to his school counselor, Mrs. Hawkins. Mrs. Hawkins greeted Memphis and reassured him that it was okay to cry. Memphis then told his counselor, "No one wants to talk to me anymore since my dad died! They just stare at me or ignore me!" Mrs. Hawkins asked Memphis why he thought that. Memphis shared, "It seemed like everyone in the class was afraid to talk to me when I walked in, so they just pretended I wasn't there." Mrs. Hawkins shared with Memphis that his classmates cared a lot about him, but they were likely afraid to upset him or say the wrong thing, so they didn't say anything at all.

Memphis responded, "I just want to be treated like a normal kid. I don't want people to be afraid to talk to me, and I don't want to talk about my dad at school." Mrs. Hawkins told him that she could not control what other students may do or say, but she could talk to his friends and encourage them to include Memphis in their normal conversations about school, sports, and video games while also asking them not to talk about his dad at school. Memphis thought that was a good plan.

As the days passed, Memphis no longer felt ignored. His friends and classmates included him in conversation and play, and school became his happy place again. Memphis was glad he told Mrs. Hawkins what he needed to feel better about coming to school.

DISCUSSION QUESTIONS

- What might Memphis have been thinking when his classmates didn't say anything when he walked into the classroom?

- What may have happened if Memphis didn't openly communicate with Mrs. Hawkins about what was bothering him?

- How do you think Memphis felt when his classmates started including him again?

- What could Memphis do if someone says or does something that hurts his feelings in the future?

PROCESSING ACTIVITY

Group processing activities allow students to remember, reflect, and find shared experiences with peers in their loss journeys.

Have students **write hurtful or upsetting comments people have said about their grief** on a sticky note or small piece of paper. Then, using a crayon, allow students to scribble through these words as hard or soft as they would like. Once scribbled through, encourage students to physically rip up the note. Remind students after they shred the note that although they can't control what other people say and do, they can control their response and what they hold on to.

ADDITIONAL ACTIVITIES

- Have students circle up and share words or actions that have been hurtful since their loss. Once everyone has had a chance to share, ask group members to share tips or strategies that have helped them move forward from that hurtful experience. Finally, have group members share words or actions that have been helpful since their loss.

- Pass out a piece of paper and coloring supplies to the group. Have students create simple signals that can help communicate their needs (like a clock for time, a hug for comfort, or a microphone for talking). Encourage students to use these symbols to explain their needs to adults or friends when they are feeling down.

CLOSING CONSIDERATIONS

Handling difficult conversations and hurtful actions while grieving can be tough. Grief can make communication challenging. It is okay to be honest about your feelings and openly communicate your needs to others in a respectful way.

To wrap up, ask students to take a moment to reflect on what they've learned about grief or something they will take away from this week's session. Then, have them summarize their thoughts in one sentence. They can share their sentence with a partner or with the whole group. If time permits, each student can also share one thing they hope to achieve or experience in the coming week.

Copy and cut out the cards for small groups to discuss. Read the cards aloud or pass out cards to students for them read during your discussion.

GRiEF SPEAK

I wish people would understand that...

One thing I wish I could say to the loved one I've lost is...

When others give me advice about grieving, I feel...

I struggle to explain how I'm feeling when...

When I talk to others about my loss, I feel...

I feel most at ease talking about my loss when...

MY COPING TOOLBOX

MIND MAP

On the board, draw a mind map and ask students to consider the meaning of *Coping*.

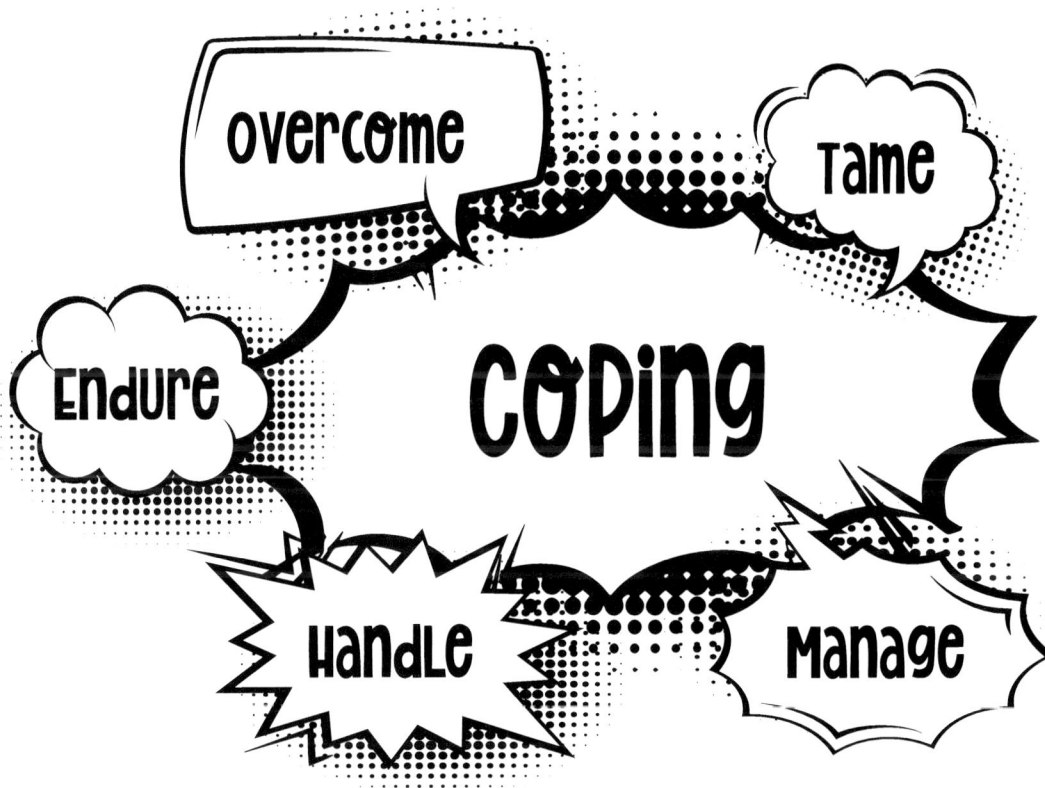

overcome

Tame

Endure

COPING

Handle

Manage

ASCA® STANDARDS

- **B-SMS 6.** Ability to identify and overcome barriers

- **B-SMS 7.** Effective coping skills

- **B-SMS 9.** Personal safety skills

- **B-SMS 10.** Ability to manage transitions and adapt to change

- Begin the group by asking members to share a rose (highlight), a thorn (lowlight), and a bud (something they are looking forward to or hoping for). Alternatively, students can use an emotion scale where they rate their feelings on a scale of 1 (very low)–10 (feeling awesome).

- Review the Group Expectations.

- Read the Lesson Introduction and ask the Circle Time Questions before reading the Story and asking the Discussion Questions. Students can work in pairs to answer the questions or individually share with the whole group.

- Complete one of the three Process Activities. If time allows, complete the Connection Cards (in pairs or a group) and the Additional Activities.

- Be sure to complete the Closing Considerations with each lesson.

LESSON INTRODUCTION

Because grief is hard and messy, it is important to explore a variety of ways to manage big grief reactions. **Coping skills** are things we can do in the moment to help us feel better and manage our feelings. Coping skills come in many forms, and often involve us using our body, thoughts, and environment to help control our responses. Just like riding a bike, utilizing coping skills in hard moments gets easier the more we practice.

CIRCLE TIME QUESTIONS

Ask students to reflect and share their answers to the following questions with the group.

- What strategies have helped you manage big feelings in the past?
- What strategies have you seen other adults or classmates use to calm down?
- What may happen if we don't use coping skills?

Sad Days and Calm Minds

Navy loved it when her class celebrated holidays and special events. Usually, these days involved parties where there were lots of treats and fun games, and her parents could come visit. One day, her teacher announced they would be having a "Goodies and Grands" day, where grandparents could come to the classroom and eat donuts with the class.

Navy instantly felt a big wave of emotion as she sat in her seat. She noticed her body get hot inside and her stomach start to tingle. Just two months ago, her grandfather had died. Navy was overwhelmed with sadness knowing her grandfather wouldn't be there. She was also afraid her grandmother wouldn't be able to come, as she lived two hours away. These thoughts made it hard for Navy to breathe.

After a moment of panic, Navy remembered a video her teacher, Ms. Austin, had shown the class a few weeks ago. The video showed them how to do something called **Square Breathing**. She thought about the video, closed her eyes, and took several big breaths in and out. Now she felt more in control of her body. Navy was relieved she could do something to help herself calm down.

When Navy went home that afternoon, she told her mom what happened. Her mom gave her a hug and told her she was proud of Navy for using a coping skill. Navy then called her grandmother, who assured her she would make the "Goodies and Grands" party.

- How do you think Navy felt when she first heard about the "Goodies and Grands" party?
- What did Navy notice happening in her body that told her she needed to use a coping skill?
- What did Navy do when she started feeling overwhelmed?
- How do you think using a coping skill helped Navy?

Group processing activities allow students to remember, reflect, and find shared experiences with peers in their loss journeys.

Utilize this time to introduce and practice the following **three coping skills** with your students by reading the following script:

"There are a lot of different coping skills we can use to help us manage our grief. Today I am going to teach you about three coping skills you can use at any time, in class or at home. After I tell you about the coping skill, we are going to practice it together."

*"The first coping skill I'm going to teach you is called **Square Breathing**. Just like Navy practiced in the story we read, square breathing is where you inhale through your nose for four seconds, hold your breath for four seconds, breathe out through your mouth for four seconds, and then pause for four seconds. You do this four times total (that's a lot of fours!). Let's practice together now:*

> *"Breathe in through your nose for four.*
>
> *"Hold for four.*
>
> *"Breathe out of your mouth for four.*
>
> *"Pause for four.*
>
> [Repeat instructions three more times]

*"The next coping skill we are going to practice is called **5,4,3,2,1**. In this skill, we are going to name five things we can see, four things we can touch, three things we can hear, two things we can smell, and one thing we love about ourselves. Let's practice by quietly thinking in our heads about:*

> *"5 things we can see.*
> [Give students 30–45 seconds to look around the room between each prompt.]
>
> *"4 things we can touch.*
>
> *"3 things we can hear.*
>
> *"2 things we can smell.*
>
> *"1 thing we love about ourselves.*
>
> *"Who can tell me: What did you see? What could you touch? Hear? Smell? What do you love about yourself?*

*"The last skill we are going to practice is called **Progressive Muscle Relaxation**. If you feel comfortable, please close your eyes. You are welcome to keep your eyes open—you can look up at the ceiling or down at your desk.*

> *"First, I want everyone to scrunch up their toes as tight as they can until I say stop.*
> [Let 5–10 seconds pass.] *Everyone stop.*
>
> *"Now I want everyone to tense up their legs as tight as they can until I say stop.*
> [Let 5–10 seconds pass.] *Everyone stop.*
>
> *"Now I want everyone to tense up their tummy as tight as they can until I say stop.*
> [Let 5–10 seconds pass.] *Everyone stop.*
>
> *"Now I want everyone to tense up their arms as tight as they can until I say stop.*
> [Let 5–10 seconds pass.] *Everyone stop.*
>
> *"Now I want everyone to tense up their face as tight as they can until I say stop.*
> [Let 5–10 seconds pass.] *Everyone stop. Slowly open your eyes when you are ready."*

Ask the group the following to wrap up the session:

- How do you feel now that you've practiced a few coping skills?

- What was your favorite coping skill and why?

- When may be a good time to practice one of these skills in the next week?

- Give each student a paper plate or paper with a large circle. Have students divide the plate or circle into "pie pieces" and label each section of the wheel with emotions they've felt since their loss. Instruct students to write or draw a simple coping strategy in each section of the wheel that can help with that emotion (Example: Sad: Listen to music.)

- Provide students with the **Coping Skills List** included in the Downloadable Resources. Ask students to highlight or circle any of the coping skills they think may be helpful and have them share with a partner what they selected and how they plan on using it in the future.

Coping Skills List

DEEP BREATHING	TALK IT OUT	DRAW OR COLOR
Practice taking slow, deep breaths to calm down. ✔ Square Breathing ✔ Belly Breathing ✔ Figure 8 Breathing	Share feelings with a trusted adult or friend.	Use art to express emotions through drawing or coloring.
JOURNALING	PLAY OUTSIDE	LISTEN TO MUSIC
Write down your thoughts and feelings in a journal.	Engage in physical activity, like walking or playing games outdoors.	Create a playlist of songs that make you feel good.
GROUNDING	POSITIVE AFFIRMATIONS	HUG A STUFFED ANIMAL
Engage your senses in the here and now by naming: 5 things you can **see** 4 things you can **touch** 3 things you can **hear** 2 things you can **smell** 1 thing you can **taste**	Repeat encouraging phrases like "I can do hard things" or "I am strong."	Cuddle a favorite stuffed animal for comfort.
PRACTICE GRATITUDE	TELL A JOKE	DO A PUZZLE
Think of three things they are thankful for each day.	Laughing can help lighten the mood.	Engage in a puzzle or activity that requires focus.
STRETCH OR MOVE	PLAY WITH PETS	VISUALIZE A HAPPY PLACE
Do some simple stretches or yoga to release tension.	Spend time with a pet for companionship and comfort.	Imagine a favorite place where you feel safe and happy.

30-MINUTE GROUPS: GRIEF
by Makenzie Perkins © National Center for Youth Issues
3

CLOSING CONSIDERATIONS

Coping skills are healthy strategies we can use to manage difficult feelings, situations, or experiences while grieving. Learning to use coping skills while having intense emotions takes time and practice.

To wrap up, ask students to take a moment to reflect on what they've learned about grief, or something they will take away from this week's session. Then, have them summarize their thoughts in one sentence. They can share their sentence with a partner or with the whole group. If time permits, each student can also share one thing they hope to achieve or experience in the coming week.

Copy and cut out the cards for small groups to discuss. Read the cards aloud or pass out cards to students for them read during your discussion.

COPING TOOLBOX

Something that always makes me feel better is...

A person I can always talk to about my feelings is...

A time I successfully used a coping skill was...

My happy place is...

A time I wish I would have used a coping skill was...

A strategy at school that helps me feel better is...

GRATITUDE IN GRIEF

MIND MAP

On the board, draw a mind map and ask students to consider the meaning of *Gratitude*.

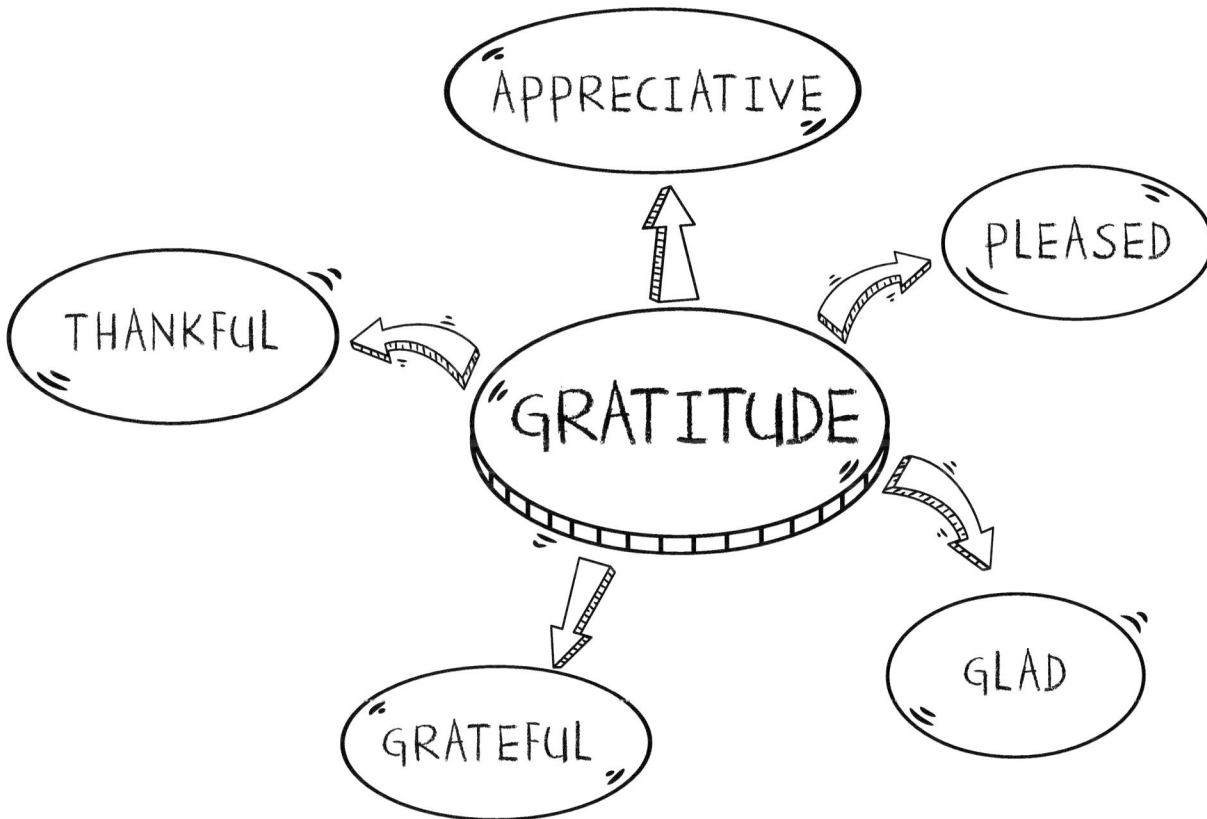

```
                    APPRECIATIVE
                         ↑
                         |
 THANKFUL  ←        GRATITUDE        →  PLEASED
                    /         \
                   ↓           ↓
              GRATEFUL        GLAD
```

ASCA® STANDARDS

- **B-SMS 6.** Ability to identify and overcome barriers

- **B-SMS 7.** Effective coping skills

- **B-SMS 10.** Ability to manage transitions and adapt to change

DIRECTIONS

- Begin the group by asking members to share a rose (highlight), a thorn (lowlight), and a bud (something they are looking forward to or hoping for). Alternatively, students can use an emotion scale where they rate their feelings on a scale of 1 (very low)–10 (feeling awesome).

ROSE	THORN	BUD
HIGHLIGHT	LOWLIGHT	I'M LOOKING FORWARD TO

- Review the Group Expectations.

- Read the Lesson Introduction and ask the Circle Time Questions before reading the Story and asking the Discussion Questions. Students can work in pairs to answer the questions or individually share with the whole group.

- Complete one of the three Process Activities. If time allows, complete the Connection Cards (in pairs or a group) and the Additional Activities.

- Be sure to complete the Closing Considerations with each lesson.

LESSON INTRODUCTION

Gratitude is feeling thankful for and appreciating the things in life that bring you joy. Sometimes when we are grieving, it is hard to remember things we are thankful for or that make us happy. Sometimes we even feel guilty about being happy. Grief and joy can co-exist, which means it is okay to feel both feelings at the same time.

Everyone has different things that help us feel gratitude. Some of us may be thankful for a place that brings us peace, like a park or a museum. Others may be grateful for a person who helps us when we are in need. No matter what we are going through, it is important to spend time each day remembering the people, places, and things that bring us joy and gratitude.

Ask students to reflect and share their answers to the following questions with the group.

- On a scale of 1 (impossible) – 5 (easy), how difficult has it been for you to find gratitude while grieving? Why?

- How has your experience with grief changed the way you appreciate people or things in your life?

- What are you most thankful for in your life right now, even while grieving?

STORY TIME

Thankful for School and Rio

Rhodes was having a rough morning. He did not want to go to school because it was the first anniversary since his best friend, Nyah, had died. He cried to his mom, begging her to stay home, but she insisted he had to go to school.

As he was walking to school, he tripped and scraped his knee. A few classmates saw what happened and laughed at him as they walked by. But one of his classmates, Rio, got off his bike and helped Rhodes up.

Once Rhodes got to school, it was time for him to complete his daily journal prompt for bell work. He looked at the board and the prompt read, "Name at least two things you are thankful for and why."

At first, Rhodes didn't write anything. He felt stuck because it was hard to think of things he was thankful for when he was missing Nyah so much. He began to think about his morning and realized he was thankful for school because that is how he met Nyah. He was also thankful for Rio, who helped him up when he fell. Thinking about both things helped Rhodes feel better.

DISCUSSION QUESTIONS

- What made it hard for Rhodes to start his journal prompt?

- How do you think Rhodes's mood may have changed after thinking about things he was thankful for?

- What do you think the classmates who walked past Rhodes when he fell could have done differently?

- How can Rhodes use gratitude, or being thankful, every day to help him feel better when missing Nyah?

PROCESSING ACTIVITY

Group processing activities allow students to remember, reflect, and find shared experiences with peers in their loss journeys.

Have students partner up and **share a person, place, and thing they are thankful for and why**. After partners have had time to discuss, circle back together as a group and allow group members to share their persons, places, and things with the rest of the group. To end the activity, have students rate how they are feeling on a scale of 1 (low) – 5 (high) after reflecting on things for which they are grateful.

ADDITIONAL ACTIVITIES

- Pass out paper and coloring supplies. Encourage group members to think of one person in their life that has been helpful in their grief journey. Once they think of a person, have each student create a thank you card for that individual. In the card, they can express ways that person has encouraged, supported, or inspired them while learning to grow around their grief. Encourage group members to deliver the cards this week if they choose.

- Pass out paper and coloring supplies. Ask every student to draw a large heart on their paper. Then, ask students to take a few moments to reflect on things they are grateful for, even on the hard days. Instruct group members to then fill their hearts with words or pictures that symbolize these things. After everyone has completed the activity, allow group members to share what they filled their hearts with.

CLOSING CONSIDERATIONS

Gratitude is about recognizing and appreciating both little and big things you are thankful for. When we practice gratitude frequently, our brains become better at recognizing the positives, even during difficult times. This can enhance our mood and mental wellness.

To wrap up, ask students to take a moment to reflect on what they've learned about grief, or something they will take away from this week's session. Then, have them summarize their thoughts in one sentence. They can share their sentence with a partner or with the whole group. If time permits, each student can also share one thing they hope to achieve or experience in the coming week.

Copy and cut out the cards for small groups to discuss. Read the cards aloud or pass out cards to students for them read during your discussion.

GRATITUDE IN GRIEF

Someone I'd like to say 'thank you' to is...

A special memory with someone I miss that makes me feel thankful is...

A time or place I struggle to think of things I'm grateful for is...

I'm thankful my loss and grief have taught me...

One thing that has happened since my loss that I'm grateful for is...

A place that reminds me of my loss and makes me feel thankful is...

Growing Around My Grief

MIND MAP

On the board, draw a mind map and ask students to consider the meaning of *Growth*.

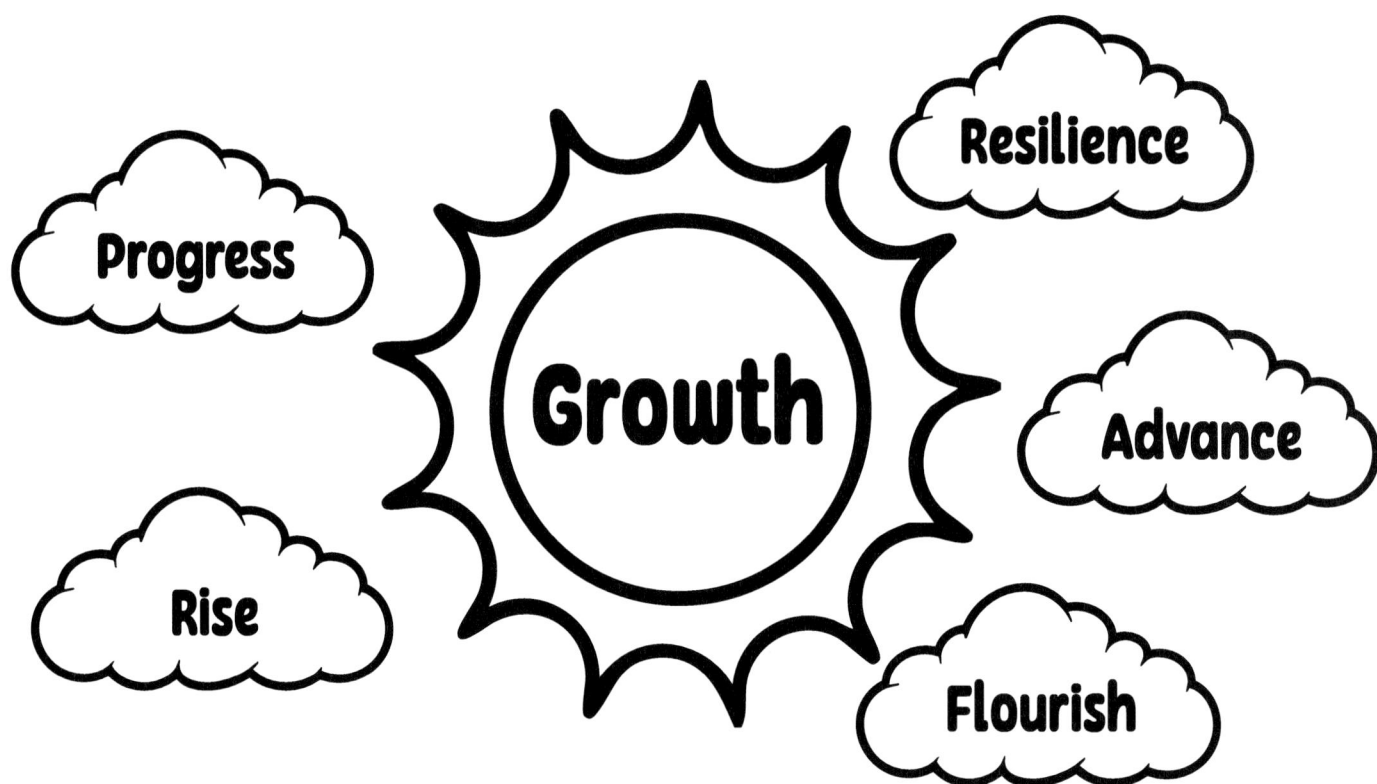

Resilience

Progress

Growth

Advance

Rise

Flourish

ASCA® STANDARDS

- **M 1.** Belief in development of whole self, including a healthy balance of mental, social/emotional and physical well-being

- **B-SMS 5.** Perseverance to achieve long and short-term goals

- **B-SMS 6.** Ability to identify and overcome barriers

- **B-SS 8.** Advocacy skills for self and others and ability to assert self, when necessary

- Begin the group by asking members to share a rose (highlight), a thorn (lowlight), and a bud (something they are looking forward to or hoping for). Alternatively, students can use an emotion scale where they rate their feelings on a scale of 1 (very low)–10 (feeling awesome).

ROSE — HIGHLIGHT | THORN — LOWLIGHT | BUD — I'M LOOKING FORWARD TO

- Review the Group Expectations.

- Read the Lesson Introduction and ask the Circle Time Questions before reading the Story and asking the Discussion Questions. Students can work in pairs to answer the questions or individually share with the whole group.

- Complete one of the three Process Activities. If time allows, complete the Connection Cards (in pairs or a group) and the Additional Activities.

- Be sure to complete the Closing Considerations with each lesson.

LESSON INTRODUCTION

Grief is something that never really goes away. Instead, as time passes, you will continue to **grow** around your grief. What this means is that some days your grief will feel as big and overwhelming as it did the first time you felt it, and other days you will hardly notice your grief, allowing space for other thoughts, emotions, and experiences. Just as your body will continue to grow bigger and stronger, so will your ability to carry and process your grief over time.

Ask students to reflect and share their answers to the following questions with the group.

- How has your grief changed over the past ten weeks?

- What is something you are proud of related to your grief journey?

- What is one way you hope you grow in your grief journey?

STORY TIME

Rosemary's Maze

Rosemary loves to write. Ever since her grandmother, Nana, had died, Rosemary has kept a journal of her feelings. Writing things down helps her feel better. One day, she wrote:

"My grief feels like a maze. I can't see the finish line. Sometimes I move forward and feel happy! Like today when I was brave and went to music class even though music class reminds me of Nana. Other days I run into obstacles, like last week when I had to celebrate my birthday without Nana here. That day made me feel like I got turned around in the maze and retraced some of my old steps where my grief felt huge. I've noticed that the more time I spend in the maze, the less scary it becomes because there are fewer surprises. I've learned that if one way doesn't work, I can always try another way to move forward. I know my Nana would be so proud of me because I always keep trying to move forward, even though some days the maze feels very tricky."

DISCUSSION QUESTIONS

- How does the metaphor of a maze help Rosemary describe her experience with grief?

- What was one way Rosemary felt like she was moving forward in her grief maze?

- What happened when Rosemary ran into an obstacle in her grief maze?

- What do you think Rosemary means when she says the maze becomes less scary over time with fewer surprises?

PROCESSING ACTIVITY

Group processing activities allow students to remember, reflect, and find shared experiences with peers in their loss journeys.

Hand out the **Grief Maze Worksheet** and ask students to note where they encounter challenges with their grief at home, at school, with friendships, and in navigating change as they find their way to the end.

Grief Maze

In the boxes, note where you've encountered challenges with your grief at home, at school, with friendships, and in navigating change.

30-MINUTE GROUPS: **GRIEF**
by Makenzie Perkins © National Center for Youth Issues

ADDITIONAL ACTIVITIES

- Using a round-robin method, allow students to share one way they believe they've grown in their grief in the past ten weeks. Once everyone has had a chance to share, allow each student to share one goal they hope to accomplish in the future as they continue to work through their grief.

- Have students write a letter to their past selves, on the day they found out about their loss. Encourage students to share with their past selves what grief may feel like, what they may notice about grief, and lessons they've learned along the way. Allow students to share their letters with the group if they would like.

CLOSING CONSIDERATIONS

Grief is not something that will go away overnight or after a certain amount of time. While grief may never fully disappear, over time you will find ways to integrate memories, embrace a wide range of emotions, and see things from a new perspective that will help you grow around your grief.

To wrap up, ask students to take a moment to reflect on what they've learned about grief, or something they will take away from this week's session. Then, have them summarize their thoughts in one sentence. They can share their sentence with a partner or with the whole group. If time permits, each student can also share one thing they hope to achieve or experience in the coming week.

Copy and cut out the cards for small groups to discuss. Read the cards aloud or pass out cards to students for them read during your discussion.

Growing Around My Grief

If I could give one piece of advice to someone who has just experienced a loss, it would be…

Looking back, I'm proud of myself for…

When I think about my grief, I hope…

One thing I do now to take care of my feelings that I didn't do before is…

Loss has taught me that it is important to…

A new strength I've discovered in myself is…

Final Group Session

LAST SESSION:
Directions and Overview

The closing group session is recommended. However, the content of this final meeting can be integrated into the tenth grief session, Growing Around My Grief, if preferred.

Directions: In this final meeting, remind group members that this will be the last time you meet as a group. Share that you will begin with the post-group survey. This survey is the same survey the group members completed during the introductory group session. Then, do one final group check-in. Close the session by having students reflect on their experiences over the past ten weeks. Pass out group completion certificates.

Post-Group Expectations: Many students will have grown accustomed to meeting with you and will need reassurance about what support will be available after the group's conclusion. Be sure to review the protocol for meeting with you once the group has concluded.

Post-Group Survey: Share with the group that the first thing they are going to complete today is the post-group survey quietly in their seats. Encourage students to complete the survey honestly and remind them there are no right or wrong answers. Once students have completed the survey, have them turn them in to you and ensure all questions have been answered.

Group Check-In: Doing one final group check-in allows for one final shared experience as a group. Ask members to share a rose (highlight), a thorn (lowlight), and a bud (something they are looking forward to or hoping for). Alternatively, students can use an emotion scale where they rate their feelings on a scale of 1 (very low) – 10 (feeling awesome).

Discussion Questions: Ask each student to reflect on their journey by exploring the following discussion questions as a group:

- What has changed for you since the first time we met?

- What is one thing you've learned about loss or grief?

- What is one thing you can do if you experience a grief burst in the future?

Closing Considerations: Thank each group member for participating in the group and congratulate them all for taking steps forward in their grief journey. Emphasize that their feelings may change over time. However, the things they learned in the group can be applied as they continue to grow around their grief. Remind them that although their loss is unique to them, they are not alone in their grief and that it is okay to ask for help in the future.

Note to Facilitators: Offer each student a small card with an encouraging message or positive affirmation to keep with them to review when having a grief burst or tough moment.

SMALL GROUP ACTION PLAN GUIDE

GRADE LEVEL

The curriculum is ideal for 2nd through 8th grade students.

GROUP TOPICS

Loss and Grief

Memories

Feelings

Naming and Taming Worries

Grief Bursts

Life Changes

Difficult Conversations

Coping Skills

Gratitude

Growth Around Grief

10-12 Group Sessions

30 MIN

CURRICULUM & MATERIALS

Curriculum:

Use this 30-Minute Groups: Grief workbook to facilitate your groups.

Materials:

Copies of surveys, worksheets, and Grief Connection Cards. Crayons, pencils, and scratch paper.

ASCA® STUDENT BEHAVIOR STANDARDS 12

B-SMS 1

B-SMS 2

B-SMS 5

B-SMS 6

B-SMS 7

B-SMS 9

B-SMS 10

B-SS 1

B-SS 2

B-SS 4

B-SS 8

M 1

NUMBER OF STUDENTS AFFECTED

A small group of 6-8 students is ideal when talking about loss and grief. These lessons can also be adapted for classroom processing sessions after a school crisis event.

PERCEPTION DATA

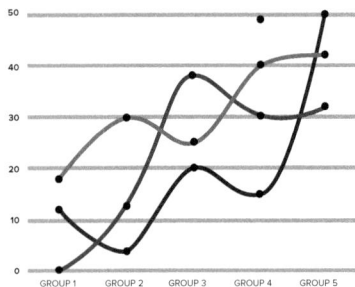

Use Grief survey data to create a visual representation of their progress using their pre- and post-group data.

OUTCOME DATA

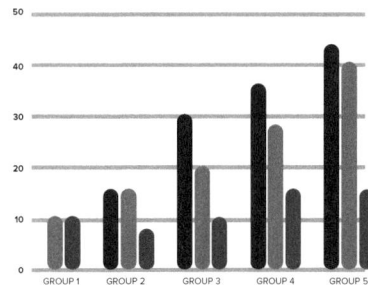

Use achievement, attendance, and behavior data to measure the progress of your students. Compare Pre- and Post-Group Surveys to determine the impact of the group lessons on students.

GRIEF GROUP
PERMISSION FORM

Greetings, Caregivers of: _____,

This form invites your student to attend a Grief Group. Our counseling department offers various services, including class lessons, small groups, and individual sessions with students. There are lots of reasons we invite students to attend groups. We invite students who might need help connecting with their peers, navigating loss and the big emotions related to grief, or simply because we think their involvement will allow them to be more successful in their education journey. Your student is not in trouble, and being part of this group is meant to be a positive time for all attendees.

This group will focus on navigating life after a loss. Specifically, we will work on processing our loss and grief, life changes, memories, feelings, grief bursts, difficult conversations, utilizing coping skills, increasing gratitude, and experiencing growth around our grief. Small groups are a fun way for students to learn valuable skills while also connecting with peers who have encountered similar challenges.

We will meet for approximately thirty minutes during the school day ____ times per week. I will work with your child's teacher to select an appropriate time that minimizes interruptions to their learning. When the students have completed all the group sessions, they will receive a Certificate of Completion.

I am excited to work with your child! Please don't hesitate to contact me with any questions or concerns.

Warm regards,

✂ -

Please complete and return by: _____

Student's Name: _____

Teacher's Name: _____

☐ YES, I agree to allow my child to attend the Grief Group.

☐ NO, I do NOT agree to allow my child to attend the Grief Group.

_____
Signature of Caregiver

GRiEF GROUP EXPECTATIONS

CONFIDENTIALITY

We know that some things are private, and not everyone needs to know about them. What is shared in the group should stay in the group, and not be repeated to anyone outside the group. However, because we are a group, we cannot promise that everyone will keep your secrets, so please be mindful of what you share with the group. If you have a major concern, you can always share it with me privately before or after the group meeting. If you share that you plan to hurt yourself or someone else, or that someone is hurting you, I will have to notify the appropriate adults to protect you.

LISTEN CAREFULLY

To listen is more than to hear. When others are speaking, we all must do our best to focus on what others say with all of our senses, refrain from interrupting, and keep our minds in the present without trying to decide what we will say next.

SHOW EVERYONE RESPECT

We show our respect for the others in our group by giving our full attention to the speaker, giving everyone a chance to talk in each group, and being safe people for one another. This means responding with curiosity, not criticism, when we think, look, or act differently than another person. This also means responding with kindness if conflict or disagreement occurs.

PARTICIPATE IN OUR GROUP ACTIVITIES

We are here to work together, so it is important that each one of us is doing our part to participate and engage. This will help us deepen our understanding of the topic, ourselves, and one another, which will enrich our learning and growth.

CREATE YOUR OWN

_____

_____

_____

_____

Group Attendance Form

Group:_____ Day/Time:_____

	1	2	3	4	5	6	7	8	9	10	11	12
DATE												
	☐	☐	☐	☐	☐	☐	☐	☐	☐	☐	☐	☐
	☐	☐	☐	☐	☐	☐	☐	☐	☐	☐	☐	☐
	☐	☐	☐	☐	☐	☐	☐	☐	☐	☐	☐	☐
	☐	☐	☐	☐	☐	☐	☐	☐	☐	☐	☐	☐
	☐	☐	☐	☐	☐	☐	☐	☐	☐	☐	☐	☐
	☐	☐	☐	☐	☐	☐	☐	☐	☐	☐	☐	☐
	☐	☐	☐	☐	☐	☐	☐	☐	☐	☐	☐	☐

SESSION 1

SESSION 2

SESSION 3

SESSION 4

SESSION 5

SESSION 6

SESSION 7

SESSION 8

SESSION 9

SESSION 10

SESSION 11

SESSION 12

Group Attendance Form (Example)

Group: 5th Grade Lunch   **Day/Time:** Thursday@12:30

	1	2	3	4	5	6	7	8	9	10	11	12
DATE	3/2	3/9	3/16	3/23								
Jane/Ms. W's Class	X	X	X	X	X	X	X	X	X	X	X	X
George/Mr. Day's Class	X	X		X	X	X	X	X	X	X	X	X
Sami/Ms. Smith's Class	X	X	X	X	X	X	X	X	X	X	X	X
John/Ms. Lee's Class	X		X	X	X	X	X	X	X	X	X	X
Malik/Ms. Lee's Class	X	X	X		X	X		X	X	X	X	X
Prishna/Ms. Smith's Class	X	X	X	X	X	X	X	X			X	X

SESSION 1	Intro/Surveys/Group Rules and Norms/ Discussed Expectations/ Connections
SESSION 2	My Grief Is Unique
SESSION 3	Life After Loss
SESSION 4	Mixed Bag of Grief
SESSION 5	Grief Bursts
SESSION 6	Ways to Remember
SESSION 7	Naming and Taming the Worries
SESSION 8	Grief Speak: Handling Difficult Conversations
SESSION 9	My Coping Toolbox
SESSION 10	Gratitude in Grief
SESSION 11	Growing Around My Grief
SESSION 12	Check-Ins/ Post-Group Survey/ Process group experience & Certificates awarded

Pre- and Post-Group Survey

My name is:_____

Date:_____

Grief Survey Pre-/Post-

Circle 👍 if the statement is **true** for you.

Circle 👎 if the statement is **NOT true** for you.

There are no right or wrong answers!

	👍	👎
I understand the difference between loss and grief.	👍	👎
I have people to talk to when I feel upset.	👍	👎
I am adjusting well to the changes in my life after my loss.	👍	👎
I understand it is natural to feel a mix of emotions while grieving.	👍	👎
I know ways to honor or remember the person/thing I lost.	👍	👎
I understand that my grief can come and go in waves.	👍	👎
I usually feel like I can ask for help when I need it.	👍	👎
I regularly use coping skills to feel better.	👍	👎
I have been able to do things I enjoy since my loss.	👍	👎
I often think about what I'm thankful for.	👍	👎
I am proud of how I have coped with my grief.	👍	👎

Anything else you would like to share about the group? Write it below.

_____

_____

Post-Group Survey Results
Grief Group Data

GROUP GOAL:

STUDENT STATEMENTS:

GPA Results

Increase the total GPA following group intervention for group participation by ____%

____%

Attendance Results

Decrease the number of absences by ____% following group intervention for group participants

____%

Discipline Results

Decrease the number of conduct referrals by ____% following group intervention

____%

STUDENTS ATTENDED

NUMBER OF SESSIONS

OVERALL IMPROVEMENT

(See Formula Lower Right)

■ Pre-Group % True   ■ Post-Group % True

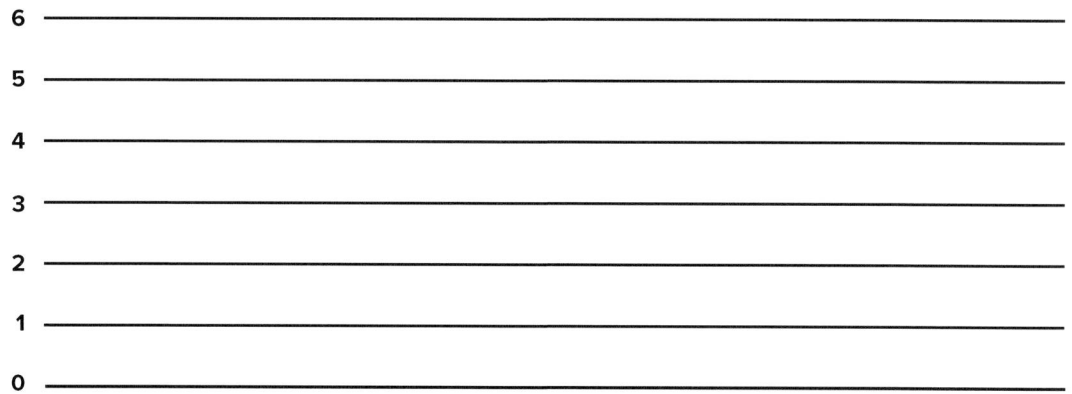

6
5
4
3
2
1
0

- I understand the difference between loss and grief.
- I have people to talk to when I feel upset.
- I am adjusting well to the changes in my life after my loss.
- I understand it is natural to feel a mix of emotions while grieving.
- I know ways to honor or remember the person/thing I lost.
- I understand that my grief can come and go in waves.
- I usually feel like I can ask for help when I need it.
- I regularly use coping skills to feel better.
- I have been able to do things I enjoy since my loss.
- I often think about what I'm thankful for.
- I am proud of how I have coped with my grief.

OVERALL IMPROVEMENT FORMULA

$$\left(\frac{\text{Post-Group Total - Pre-Group Total}}{\text{Pre-Group Total}} \right) \times 100$$

Grief Group Data

GROUP GOAL:

TBD

STUDENT STATEMENTS:

TBD

GPA Results

Increase the total GPA following group intervention for group participation by __5__ %

__5__ %

Attendance Results

Decrease the number of absences by __53__ % following group intervention for group participants

__53__ %

Discipline Results

Decrease the number of conduct referrals by __42__ % following group intervention

__42__ %

STUDENTS ATTENDED

6

NUMBER OF SESSIONS

12

OVERALL IMPROVEMENT

63.15%

(See Formula Lower Right)

Pre-Group % True ▮ Post-Group % True ▮

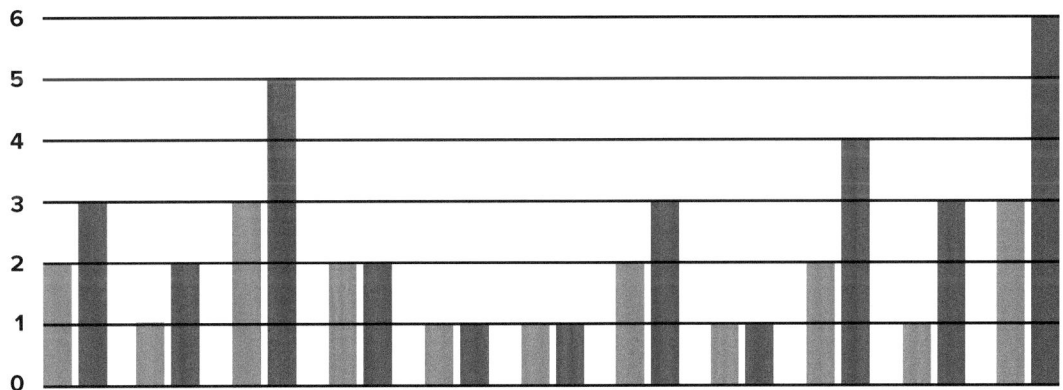

Chart categories:
- I understand the difference between loss and grief.
- I have people to talk to when I feel upset.
- I am adjusting well to the changes in my life after my loss.
- I understand it is natural to feel a mix of emotions while grieving.
- I know ways to honor or remember the person/thing I lost.
- I understand that my grief can come and go in waves.
- I usually feel like I can ask for help when I need it.
- I regularly use coping skills to feel better.
- I have been able to do things I enjoy since my loss.
- I often think about what I'm thankful for.
- I am proud of how I have coped with my grief.

OVERALL IMPROVEMENT FORMULA AND CALCULATION

$$\left(\frac{\text{Post-Group Total} - \text{Pre-Group Total}}{\text{Pre-Group Total}} \right) \times 100$$

$$\left(\frac{31 - 19}{19} \right) \times 100 \qquad \left(.6315 \right) \times 100 = 63.15\%$$

30-MINUTE GROUPS

CERTIFICATE
OF COMPLETION

This Certificate is Presented to:

_____

For Participating in the **Grief Group!**

Facilitator: _____

WOO-HOO!

GRIEF GROUP
COMPLETION LETTER

Date:_____

Hello!

Today was the final session in our Grief Group, and we wanted to let you know that your student has been presented with a Certificate of Completion. Over our time together, we have reviewed the following topics:

- My Grief Is Unique

- Life After Loss

- Mixed Bag of Grief

- Grief Bursts

- Ways to Remember

- Naming and Taming the Worries

- Grief Speak: Handling Difficult Conversations

- My Coping Toolbox

- Gratitude in Grief

- Growing Around My Grief

I am still available to your student as needed in the future. However, we will no longer be meeting every week. Please feel free to contact me with any questions or concerns.

I am so proud of your student and excited they were able to attend. Thank you so much for allowing them to participate in our Grief Group!

Warm regards,

_____

School Counselor

THE RESOURCES IN THIS BOOK ARE AVAILABLE FOR YOU AS A DIGITAL DOWNLOAD!

Please visit **ncyi.org/30mingrief** to access the downloadable resources.

Enter the code below to unlock the resources:

GRIEF565

ABOUT THE AUTHOR

Makenzie Perkins, M.S., currently serves as the Counseling and Threat Assessment Supervisor for Collierville Schools in Tennessee, where she coordinates school counseling, threat assessment, and crisis response. Previously, she was the Prevention Counselor at Collierville High School, supporting students and staff through complex mental health challenges and crises at Tennessee's largest high school. No stranger to loss and grief, Makenzie personally navigated the death of her sister while in high school, an experience that both shaped her and fuels her passion for this work. A National Certified Counselor, she holds both a Master of Science and Clinical Mental Health Specialist degree from the University of Memphis. Additionally, she is a Certified Master Trainer in Behavioral Threat Assessment through the Department of Homeland Security. Makenzie is dedicated to equipping professionals with essential skills in grief support, threat assessment, crisis management, and addressing the ever-changing mental health needs of today's youth.

thecrisiscounselor.org

A Brief Look at Makenzie's Workshop Sessions

The Colors of Loss: 10 Expressive Counseling Techniques that Work

Did you know new studies estimate 1 in 12 children will lose a parent or sibling before the age of 18? This presentation will allow school counselors to leave with creative ways to help students process their own grief journeys. A variety of expressive counseling techniques will be explored (and practiced!) that can be utilized in both individual and group sessions for all ages. Although we can't control if a student experiences loss and grief, we can help give their grief a voice.

Connecting the Dots: A Deep Dive into K-12 Threat Assessment

Curious if your school or district is prepared to prevent and manage potential acts of targeted violence? Wondering how different professionals in a school should be utilized to build a functioning multidisciplinary threat assessment team? Look no further! Using a variety of case studies and tabletop exercises, participants will leave with a better understanding of targeted violence, take an in-depth look at the threat assessment process, and learn how to implement a variety of interventions to effectively enhance school safety. This training workshop is designed to last 3-5 hours and can be used as a starter course or modified as a training refresher for school professionals with an already established threat assessment team.

Beyond the Screen: Responding Effectively to Suicidal Ideation

School counselors are uniquely positioned to be front line responders to students presenting in crisis. This workshop is designed to enhance a school counselor's knowledge on current suicide statistics, explore strategies to provide effective screening, and demonstrate how to create meaningful safety plans. Special emphasis will be placed on empowering student voice through this process.

Making Minutes for Mental Health

Whether you are a school counselor overwhelmed with the mental health needs of your caseload, or a parent wondering how on earth you can help your child navigate the ever-changing world we live in, this session is for you. Participants will gain a better understanding of current mental health trends, how to recognize declining mental wellness, and hands on techniques to support students experiencing a variety of mental health challenges.

The Four Pillars of Prevention

Addressing increasing rates of violent, threatening, and concerning behavior present challenges for school leaders across the nation. This workshop is designed to explore four essential pillars of prevention, including emergency planning, physical security, school climate, and community connectedness and how they all play a major role in school safety. Post-incident reviews and case studies will be explored to help participants brainstorm current gaps and areas of growth in their own school safety plans in this hands-on session.

ncyionline.org/speakers

NATIONAL CENTER for
YOUTH ISSUES

About NCYI

National Center for Youth Issues provides educational resources, training, and support programs to foster the healthy social, emotional, and physical development of children and youth. Since our founding in 1981, NCYI has established a reputation as one of the country's leading providers of teaching materials and training for counseling and student-support professionals. NCYI helps meet the immediate needs of students throughout the nation by ensuring those who mentor them are well prepared to respond across the developmental spectrum.

Connect With Us Online!

f

@nationalcenterforyouthissues

(Twitter)

@ncyi

(Instagram)

@nationalcenterforyouthissues